SEPTEMBER–

Guidelines

VOLUME 16 / PART 3

Edited by **Grace Emmerson and John Parr**

The Bible Reading Fellowship
OPENING THE BIBLE

Writers in this issue

Joshua **Michael Tunnicliffe** is Director of Studies for the Northern Ordination Course. He served previously as a Methodist minister in Stoke-on-Trent and Birmingham. He is the author of *Chronicles to Nehemiah* in the BRF *People's Bible Commentary* series.

Living Jubilee **Rebecca Dudley** is Adult Christian Education Adviser at Christian Aid. She is ordained in the Presbyterian Church USA and affiliated with the United Reformed Church in England.

Jesus in Paul's letters **James Dunn** is Lightfoot Professor of Divinity in the University of Durham. A leading British New Testament scholar, he is the author of many books and articles, most recently *The Theology of Paul the Apostle*, T&T Clark, 1998.

Habakkuk **Enid Mellor** is a specialist in Religious Education and has had many years' experience of teaching in schools, colleges of education and university departments of education, including King's College, London. She is the author of *Proverbs* in the BRF *People's Bible Commentary* series.

A month for remembering **John Parr** is Canon of St Edmundsbury Cathedral and Continuing Ministerial Education Officer in the Diocese of St Edmundsbury and Ipswich.

The Gospel of Matthew **Elizabeth Raine** is a minister of the Word in the Uniting Church in Australia, and works for the Board of Social Responsibility in Sydney. She has worked in education, health care, student chaplaincy and theological education. She is currently completing her doctoral research on the Gospel of Matthew for the University of Durham.

Psalms for Advent **John Eaton**, formerly Reader in Old Testament Studies in the University of Birmingham, has published several works on Old Testament subjects, including *The Circle of Creation: Animals in the Light of the Bible* (SCM Press).

Christmas and New Year **Graham Kings** is the founding Director of the Henry Martyn Centre for the Study of Mission and World Christianity, Westminster College, Cambridge, and an affiliated lecturer in the Faculty of Divinity. He is an honorary Canon of Kerugoya Cathedral, Kenya, taught theology at St Andrew's College, Kabare 1985–91 and was a curate in Harlesden, London. He has published various articles and poems, and is a contributing editor of the *International Bulletin of Missionary Research*.

THE GUIDELINES
Magazine

The BRF Prayer

O God our Father,
in the holy scriptures
you have given us your word
to be our teacher and guide:
help us and all the members of our Fellowship
to seek in our reading
the guidance of the Holy Spirit
that we may learn more of you
and of your will for us,
and so grow in likeness to your Son,
Jesus Christ our Lord.
Amen.

Editors' Letter

Continuing the millennium theme of a new start, this issue opens with readings from Joshua, which tells of Israel's entry into its promised land. These stories of success and failure are packed with human emotion, as well as a ruthlessness which modern readers find offensive—but how like today's world! Michael Tunnicliffe shows us how this disturbing book can challenge us and open windows on to our own situation.

Many people hoped that the year 2000 would mark a new start for the world's poor, burdened as they are by crippling debt. Rebecca Dudley, of Christian Aid, reminds us of the inseparability of our worship of God and concern for our neighbour. Her reflections on 'Living Jubilee' show how the campaign for debt relief is rooted in both Old and New Testaments.

Professor James Dunn is a leading British New Testament scholars. We welcome him as a new *Guidelines* contributor. His notes on Jesus in Paul's letters complete our series on Jesus for the new millennium. They focus on the heart of Paul's understanding of Jesus—his death and resurrection—and go on to explore the ramifications of his faith in the crucified and risen Christ.

Habakkuk is hardly one of the most popular books in the Bible. It comes from turbulent times, telling of a prophet's journey from fear to faith as he lays hold on God in prayer. Enid Mellor's notes illuminate its background and message. Sandwiched between Habakkuk and Elizabeth Raine's second instalment of notes on Matthew (which is surely up there in the top ten!) is a week of notes for the beginning of November, a month in which the church is particularly encouraged to attend to the business of Remembrance.

We go into Advent with John Eaton's selected psalms. His notes help us to share with the psalmist in waiting trustfully and joyfully on the Lord, for ourselves and for those who suffer, as we approach the joy of Christmas. This year's Christmas readings are by Graham Kings. Their theme (God's mission) might at first sight appear unusual—as is their largely poetic style—but on further reflection we can see how it encapsulates the message of Christmas, when we celebrate God's sending his Son into the world. Though the notes make little direct reference to Christmas, they do shed fresh light on the significance and impact of the coming of Jesus.

We greatly value the letters we continue to receive. It's good to know that these notes mean so much to you—as one reader put it, they are 'one of the highlights of the day'. Your comments help us in planning future notes, and strengthen the sense of fellowship we share as students of the Word of God.

Grace Emmerson, John Parr (Guidelines Editors)

Common Worship: new services for the Church of England

Rachel Boulding

*C*ommon Worship: Services and Prayers for the Church of England is a new collection of worship resources which are being published this autumn. Last year, the Methodist Church produced a new worship book, while other churches, such as the Roman Catholic Church, have also been revising their services.

For the Church of England, the new material will replace *The Alternative Service Book 1980* (ASB) from 1 January 2001. The ASB has come to the end of its period of use: it was always designed to be temporary and now, after twenty years, its weaknesses as well as its strengths have become apparent. The Church decided that there was a need to revise the ASB, so that it could continue to draw on both modern and traditional services. The result is *Common Worship*—services which bring together the best of both ancient and modern, classic and contemporary.

The Book of Common Prayer

The best of both ancient and modern

(BCP, sometimes known as '1662', the traditional service book originally compiled in the sixteenth century) is authorized permanently and is completely untouched by this revision process. However, the main services from it, slightly adapted to reflect the way they are commonly used today, will now take their place alongside modern services as part of the *Common Worship* range.

Why do we need new services?

Our world is constantly changing and our understanding of God is always developing. God may not change, but in every generation we find new ways of expressing ourselves to one another and to God. When the Church of England's only forms of service were those in The Book of Common Prayer, worship was theoretically fixed for hundreds of years. Yet people found other ways of adding variety and expressing themselves: they added hymns and songs; they added extra ceremony and actions; and they added extra services and festivals, such as Christmas Carol Services, Remembrance Sunday and Harvest Festival.

Over the past few decades there has been a great deal of thinking and experimentation with new services across all churches. This has continued in recent years and has culminated in the latest round of new worship materials.

Classic and contemporary

One of the most striking aspects of *Common Worship* is that it contains both traditional and modern language forms of service, side by side. It signals an end to the rigid separation of ancient and modern. When the *ASB* was introduced, containing almost entirely modern language material, the confidence that the Church had in it led some to feel that traditional services in The Book of Common Prayer were being undervalued and that we were in danger of losing a vital part of our heritage.

The *Common Worship* services, by contrast, show that both BCP and modern services have a valued place in the Church today and are part of the Church's future, not just its past. The Church has learned from twenty years' use of the *ASB* and selected the best parts of it to go into the new materials. Some services, such as the modern form of Holy Communion (called Order One and similar to Rite A), are not greatly changed from *ASB*. Other parts of *ASB* which have not stood the test of time, such as the Funeral services, have been revised more extensively. So:

- The new services bring together the best of the traditional services, the best of *ASB* and some newly written material;

- The main volume of *Common Worship* contains both modern services and services based on BCP, including forms of Holy Communion and Morning and Evening Prayer;

- All key texts (such as the Creeds, the Lord's Prayer, *Gloria in Excelsis*, the Prayer of Humble Access, Canticles, the Litany and so on) are available in both modern and traditional language forms;

- The inbuilt flexibility in *Common Worship* services allows local churches to make appropriate choices and to mix modern and traditional texts within one service (so that, for example, texts such as the Lord's Prayer and the Creed can be said or sung in traditional forms, even when the rest of the service is in modern language).

Connections

Common Worship emphasizes the structure of each service, within which local churches will be able to choose the materials which are most suitable for their ministry and community. At the beginning of each service, an outline structure is printed, so that it is easy to see how the different parts fit together. Churches will be able to choose between a wider range of prayers, such as intercessions, and from a wider choice of seasonal provisions. So:

- By permitting local flexibility within a common framework, the new services make connections with both the local context and the wider Church;

- By including both the classic and the contemporary, the new services connect with the Church's heritage and with its future;

- The provision for local decisions and choices reflects a confidence in local church leaders to know best which forms of worship are most appropriate for the context in which a given church is set.

The main service book

The main Common Worship service book will contain:

- Holy Communion Services (in four forms, following both BCP and ASB patterns in both modern and traditional language);

- Morning and Evening Prayer for Sundays (in modern and BCP forms);

- A form of Night Prayer (Compline) in both traditional and modern language;

- Baptism;

- Thanksgiving for the Gift of a Child;

- Calendar, Lectionary tables and Collects;

- Some seasonal material, prayers for various occasions, the litany and other resources;

- The Psalms, in a new translation designed specifically for use in worship.

The book deliberately does not include printed-out Bible readings, which took up much of the *ASB*. Nor does it contain occasional services. The intention is to have a more manageable worship book which will be shorter than the *ASB* but still contain the essentials of Church of England prayer.

Other key services

The Marriage, Funeral and Wholeness and Healing services will also be published this autumn, in a separate book of Pastoral Services. Within the next few years, further material will be published, such as services for Daily Prayer. Services for Christmas, Easter and other times of year, which are currently available in books such as Lent, Holy Week, Easter and The Promise of

His Glory are being put into a single *Times and Seasons* volume.

As well as the main books, there will also be a number of services published as booklets and cards. These include Holy Communion, Baptism, Marriage and Funeral. There will also be a large format President's edition, a desk edition, leather-bound presentation volumes and some services available in large print.

Quality and cost

The aim is to ensure that every aspect of the content, design and presentation of the new services is of the highest quality. This is in keeping with the belief that in worship we should offer God our very best. The *Common Worship* services in all formats are tools to facilitate excellent worship at the local level.

Tools to facilitate excellent worship

The Church also recognizes that many churches are under very tough financial constraints. The aim is to enable every church to have access to excellent resources. This has been done by keeping the cost of the books as low as possible, consistent with the aim for a good-quality product that will stand the test of time. The most frequently used services will be produced in the form of affordable booklets. Furthermore, all the services will be available in electronic form on disk and on the Internet (the latter for free) to make it easier for local churches to produce their own printed orders of service. Many will choose to keep costs down by producing booklets specially for their own congregation for at least some of the services, perhaps also buying a smaller number of copies of the books.

The publishing is being done by the Church's own publications arm, Church House Publishing, so that the process can be monitored closely and costs kept within reach of parishes. The aim of the publishing process is not to generate large profits, but to cover costs. Any surpluses generated will be returned to the Church, rather than going to private publishing houses.

What matters most

What matters most is the next step: churches using *Common Worship* in ways that fit the local situation, turning words into living worship. There will be decisions to be taken: each church will need to work out how it uses the new materials in its own way. It is hoped that people will take the opportunities offered by the new services to re-think, renew and refresh their worship. The aim is to glorify God and to connect our worship with the worship of every time and every place—and with the never-ending worship in heaven.

Rachel Boulding is Senior Liturgy Editor at Church House Publishing. The article draws on material prepared by the Revd Mark Earey, Praxis National Education Officer.

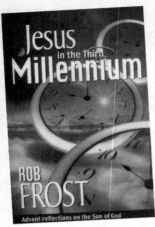

Jesus in the Third Millennium

In today's secularized world, Christians need a clear understanding of who Jesus is, in order to share his love with others. *Jesus in the Third Millennium*, BRF's Advent book for 2000, presents a user-friendly introduction to the person of Jesus. It is a time of preparing for Jesus, so what better time for coming to a richer understanding of who he is? The book's author is Rob Frost, National Evangelist for the Methodist Church in the UK, and leader of Easter People, an annual Christian holiday for over 10,000 people.

Jesus: The Alpha and the Omega

To him who loves us and has freed us from our sins by his blood, and has made us to be a kingdom and priests to serve his God and Father—to him be glory and power for ever and ever! Amen.

> *Look, he is coming with the clouds,*
>   *and every eye will see him,*
> *even those who pierced him;*
>   *and all the peoples of the earth will*
>   *mourn because of him.*
>   *So shall it be! Amen.*

'I am the Alpha and the Omega' says the Lord God, 'who is, and who was, and who is to come, the Almighty.'

(Revelation 1:5b–8, NIV)

The Advent season is a time for looking back. We look back to the start of all things and remember that Jesus Christ has been at work from the very beginning. He was there at creation, and the very life of the planet emanates from him.

In the beginning was the Word, and the Word was with God, and the Word was God. He was with God in the beginning (John 1:1).

The Advent season is a time for looking around us. As we wonder at all that Christ is doing in and among his people, we recognize that in some mysterious way he is working his purposes out all around us. And we see only a glimpse of what he is doing right now, for he is moving in ways far beyond our understanding.

We see only a glimpse of what he is doing

In him all things hold together (Colossians 1:17).

But perhaps most of all, the Advent season is a time for looking forward. It's a time to recognize that Jesus is the Alpha and the Omega, the beginning and the end of everything. His purposes are working towards an ending and a conclusion.

The famous preacher Leslie Weatherhead gathered congregations of many hundreds at the famous City Temple church in London every week. Looking back over forty years of ministry, he wondered at how God's purposes were being worked out through it all. He wrote:

Man's heart trembles for fear at the very discoveries of power which he himself has made. Belief in God seems often on the wane and men wonder what the end will be. The Christian message is that the climax of history will be worthy of the Creator, that a strong hand is in control, that the string of events we call history will not end in meaninglessness, or run out like a stream in the desert, but that Christ will reign and His promises be fulfilled. (*Over His Own Signature*, Epworth Press, 1955)

Many people look to the future of the planet with uncertainty, and even with fear. They talk with depressing urgency about the way that everything is getting worse, and fear that tomorrow can only be inferior to today. But those of us who are Christians have turned over the last page of history. We know the end of the story. And we know that Jesus is there in victory at the end of all things!

The late Dr Donald English once told a story I've never forgotten. He was taken to a wrestling match by his son to see an international contest. He described the experience in vivid detail, and described a particular bout which ran completely out of control.

A wrestler, dressed all in black and with an evil-looking mask, beat his smaller opponent to the ground. He refused to obey the referee, and continued to attack his prey with ferocious force. When the referee tried to intervene, this wrestler threw him out of the ring. No one was there to help, and it seemed that evil was victorious.

But then, without warning, the famous wrestler 'Big Daddy' strode down the aisle and mounted the ring. He cast out the black-hooded fighter, brought the referee back into the ring, and helped the beaten man to his feet. Order was restored, evil was vanquished, good was victorious.

Jesus is there in victory at the end of all things!

Dr English didn't need to expound the story. The meaning was clear. The Omega had arrived.

'Behold, I am coming soon! My reward is with me, and I will give to everyone according to what he has done. I am the Alpha and the Omega, the First and the Last, the Beginning and the End' (Revelation 22:12–13).

The book of Revelation is the completion of the book of Genesis. In Genesis we read of the creation of the old heavens and earth, of Satan's first deeds, of human beings cast out of Paradise and of the new dominance of sin and death.

In Revelation we read of a new heaven and earth, of Satan cast into hell, believers entering paradise and the destruction of sin and death. The Omega has arrived!

As you look out on the start of a new day, welcome Him as the Alpha—the beginning—and commit it to him. And at the end of the day, recognize that he is the Omega—the ending—and offer it to him.

As you begin a new project, invite him in at the start... and when it's over, thank him at the end. Recognize that your life isn't just a random sequence of incidents, events and meetings. You are part of the significant flow of beginnings and endings which is the will of Christ.

Advent is a time to rejoice that he is working his purposes out through the days of our lives and that on the last day we will see the culmination of all his wonderful work in us.

Corrie ten Boom, the little Dutch Christian who spent some dark years in the Ravensbrück concentration camp, was once making an intricate needlework pattern. She held it up for all to see, and it was just a jumble of threads and colours. 'Look at this,' she said. 'It makes no sense at all. It looks like life!' But then she turned the needlework over, and revealed a beautifully threaded pattern which spelt 'God is love'. 'One day,' she said, 'we'll see it from the side of the One to whom it all makes sense!'

Jesus is the Alpha and the Omega, the Beginning and the End. He is taking the tangled threads of our lives and weaving them into his perfect will. He is taking the confusing strands of who we are and fusing them into the purposes of his love. This Advent, let's discover that there is an Ending! Let's run with excitement towards the finishing line! Let's recognize that when we get there, he will be there to meet us!

My Father, I am so thankful that you have no beginning and no end—that you dwell outside the limits of time, in eternity! You know how easily I'm weighted down by the 'urgent' things that occupy my time and keep me from living with eternity in view. Create in me today a sense of your eternal life and love. Lift my sights above this thin, fragile, passing ribbon of time and set my foot on the solid granite path to eternity.

David Hazard, *Early Will I Seek You*,
Bethany House Publishers, 1991

To order this book, go to page 159.

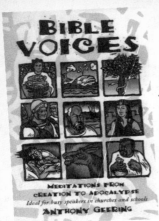

BIBLE VOICES

MEDITATIONS FROM
CREATION TO APOCALYPSE
Ideal for busy speakers in churches and schools
ANTHONY GEERING

Bible Voices

*B*ible Voices is a collection of mono-
logues which bring to vivid life the
people and events of the Bible, both
great and small. They can be read as
meditations, or shared with a group
for discussion. But the book is chiefly
designed to provide ideal material for
inspiring presentations at church
services, school assemblies or even
after-dinner speeches! Author
Anthony Geering is Rector of Crediton, Devon. Read on for
an unusual approach to the Christmas story and a darkly
humorous look at Queen Jezebel.

Department of Health, Province of Judea

Dear Sir,

A recent inspection of your
property known as 'The Key of
David' Public House, situated in
the town of Bethlehem within this
province, found you in breach of
government regulations.

On the night of 24 December,
your inn, with licensed accommo-
dation available for a maximum of
thirty persons, had approximately
seventy-six people sleeping on the
premises. Our Inspector was told
that forty-six of these individuals
were members of your family.
However, the recently completed
census clearly shows that your family consists of five people.

Whilst visiting the town, our
Inspector received a quantity of
complaints from your immediate
neighbours of music played at an
unacceptable volume for a built-up
area. As one informant put it, the
music 'seemed to fill the whole
sky'. May we remind you that your
licence does not extend to music
and dancing.

You are further accused of
exceeding the prescribed licensing
hours for serving intoxicating bev-
erages. As you are no doubt aware,
summonses have been issued for
out-of-hours drinking to a number
of your patrons, including several
shepherds employed by the munic-

ipality to watch over their flocks by night.

However, this notification is chiefly concerned with the fact that our Inspector found a newborn baby in a part of the inn reserved for domestic animals. Apart from the obvious disregard for basic hygiene, further investigation adduced the information that no midwife attended the birth, that the parents were itinerants, and that the said stable or cowshed was visited by foreign people without valid immunization certificates.

It is our duty to warn you that we shall be applying for a closure notice on your business and that a substantial fine will be levied for the above breaches of health and safety regulations.

Yours faithfully…

Jezebel's last morning

You see, darling, I'm supposed to be terribly wicked, but really I'm just your average queen. Not too much off over the ears, please, and I'll have the manicure now.

It's that man, that prophet—he spreads lies about me. First it was Elijah. Now it's the other one, Elisha. Troublemakers. Oh, and of course that po-faced Micaiah. He's a sly one. I'd like to wipe all their names off the fixtures list. Look at what they're doing now—trying to make Jehu king. Do they think I don't know that's going on? Daddy always said, don't mix religion and politics. Keep the religious people sweet, he said, but keep them in their place.

Trouble with these prophets is, they think their God's got some sort of monopoly. Then they go on as if they're in charge and not my son, Joram. They were a regular epidemic a few years ago and we sorted them. It's time for another prophet purging, don't you think? Once this war's over, Elisha is going to regret dabbling with Damascus and juggling with Jehu.

I'll have some of that dark henna, sweetie. And get a move on. Something's going to happen today. I feel it in my bones. Jehu won't attack Jezreel—nice, big, strong tower here. With a bit of luck and the help of Baal, we can surprise him and avenge Ahab, my husband. He was a good king, if a bit weak. That business over the vineyard. What was the fellow's name? Naboth. I ask you, darling, who's in charge here, king or prophet?

That's nice. Leave it like that. If Jehu, that Zimri, should come calling here at the House of Ivory, I think we can handle him.

Now, how do I look?

I feel drop dead gorgeous…

To order this book, go to page 159.

BRF Ministry

In recent years, BRF has devoted energy to publishing books to complement the three regular series of Bible reading notes. Now, alongside the publishing we are developing the wider 'ministry' of BRF once again. We want to engage with people where they are—individuals, groups, churches, local communities—and have set aside people in the BRF team who are dedicated to developing this 'down to earth' ministry.

Ministry among children—Sue Doggett

Since January 1999, Sue Doggett has been developing BRF's ministry among children alongside her work as a commissioning editor, and now divides her time equally between these two roles.

Sue has worked at BRF since February 1994, joining initially to work on the adult books with Shelagh Brown. Previously she had run her own audio recording company from home and one of her first roles at BRF was to record audio-cassettes for publication alongside the books. An early project was a cassette of music and words to accompany *What's in a Word?* by David Winter. A historical note: Sue started her career in Religious Broadcasting at the BBC, where she worked as David's PA on the *Sunday* programme!

As well as her broadcasting work, Sue had always been interested in working with children. When her own two daughters were young, she was very involved with their primary school, helping out in the classroom and, as a member of the PTA, producing, script-writing and performing in their school pantomimes for seven successive years! Before she joined BRF she was also involved in running a Brownie Pack for five years. All this experience came to the fore when she got the chance to work on what became the first *Barnabas* title for BRF.

Barnabas books

BRF had been planning to start developing children's books, once the adult book range was established. When a book on holiday clubs was offered to BRF by Mike Fox, Sue felt it needed further work and helped him rewrite it. It was published as *The Christian Adventure* and in 1995 the *Barnabas* list was launched.

Since then, *Barnabas* has gone from strength to strength, establishing its identity as a range of books that open up the Bible for children. The seasonal activity books have proved an especially popular feature, and September brings *The Christmas Tree's Tale* by Stephanie Jeffs, while in November comes *The Road to Easter* by Jacqui Gardner and Chris Leonard. Both books offer crafts, games and Bible-based thoughts for children.

Barnabas books are now divided into four strands: storytelling, Bible reading, prayer and spirituality, and teaching resources. It is via these four strands that the development of *Barnabas* ministry has taken place, working with schools and churches around the country, offering workshops, assemblies and presentations. Sue is working with professional actors and storytellers, as well as BRF authors, to prepare the presentations, with the agenda of bringing the Bible alive for children, whatever their starting point.

Barnabas has gone from strength to strength

Barnabas Live

Barnabas Live is an innovative presentation being offered to schools, libraries and theatres throughout England during 2000. It offers a full day of storytelling followed by creative activities and workshops that take the themes of the story a little further. For schools, the National Curriculum with its demand for literacy and RE teaching offers ways in for *Barnabas Live*, and the *Barnabas* books provide a rich resource of material for the programmes to draw on.

Training children's workers

Sue, a licensed Lay Reader in the Church of England, has also been planning with church networks to set up training events to help and equip those who work with children in Sunday Schools and after-school clubs. A typical day's programme for these workshops might include how to plan events, how to use the Bible, craft and games ideas, creative ways of teaching prayer, and how to plan ahead strategically.

As an experienced Sunday School teacher, who helped to build a team of co-workers from scratch at her local church, Sue is well aware of the challenges and opportunities posed by working with children in church:

> It's so important to get people excited about teaching children, and I know it can be a steep learning curve for many people—discovering how to keep children's attention, how to find the right level at which to speak and tailor a programme to the needs of your group. What is so important, though, is helping children link church and Christianity with having a good time. That's the aim behind so much of what we are planning with BRF's Barnabas ministry.

Ministry among adults—Anne Hibbert

Since BRF was founded in 1922, we have been helping individuals and congregations to encounter the living God through regular Bible reading and prayer, so that they grow spiritually and become more effective as disciples. Throughout much of our history, we have been involved with the local church, with BRF staff working with clergy, groups, and individuals, offering training, advice and practical help in the areas of Bible reading and spiritual growth.

In July 1999, the Revd Anne Hibbert accepted BRF's invitation to become our first Mission and Spirituality Adviser, heading up BRF's ministry among adults.

After finishing a job at the Church of England Millennium Office, she wanted to move on to work that would use what she felt was her primary gift—evangelism, helping people to encounter God for the first time. When she found out more about the ministry opportunities unfolding at BRF, she realized that this could be the right move for her:

> BRF is a small organization with a big vision. Its mission statement about helping people to encounter God through prayer and Bible study speaks about what is close to my own heart.

Before joining the Millennium Office, Anne had worked as Evangelism Co-ordinator and Adviser for seven and a half years at CPAS, one of the leading ministry agencies and resource providers for the Church of England. As part of her evangelistic work, she taught the Lost for Words course which James Lawrence later wrote up as a book, published by BRF last year.

Working with people

Anne's role as BRF's Mission and Spirituality Adviser builds on her love of working with people by keeping her 'on the road', travelling round to churches and church related groups, preaching, speaking and interacting with members old and new. She also organizes BRF's programme of retreats and quiet days, aiming to cover more and more of Britain as her work develops.

While part of her role is to make people aware of the books BRF has to offer, promoting books is secondary to her main focus of helping people encounter God. She is keen to emphasize that she is not part of the publishing team in any way.

I was able to draw up my own job description when I joined BRF, with no writing involved as I much prefer dealing with people. A lot of people think that BRF is just a publisher, producing books, but my work is to get us involved in ministry in a much more grass-roots way.

Retreats are increasingly popular for all kinds of people—not just churchgoers! Anne is keen to develop opportunities for those who want to take time out for God but who perhaps cannot afford the luxury of two or three days away from home and work. A 'quiet day' may be easier to manage two or three times a year, and can be just as helpful if the time available is carefully structured.

Anne is already involved in networks such as Reaching the Unchurched, Christian Viewpoint (a movement concerned to reach unchurched women with a gospel message) and the Evangelical Alliance. She is also part of the planning group for EA's conference in November 2001, where she will have responsibility for the discipleship part of the programme. In 1994, she was among the first women to be ordained priest in the Church of England.

Future opportunities

BRF Chief Executive Richard Fisher says that both these areas of ministry being developed by Anne and Sue offer tremendously exciting opportunities.

It offers us a way of bringing what BRF has to offer to an even wider audience. Unsurprisingly, though, the financial costs involved are not insignificant. We need the help of BRF readers and supporters if we are to secure our current activities and take BRF's ministry forward. With their help, there is so much more that we could do.

If you would like to support BRF's ministry, the response form on page 155 sets out a number of ways in which you can do so. Please complete the form and send it back to us here at BRF.

If you would like further information about any of the initiatives or programmes mentioned above, or if you would like to contact Sue or Anne about their work, please write to them at BRF.

The People's Bible Commentary

First published on its own in 1996, John Fenton's *Galatians* commentary has been fully revised and extended for the new edition published last autumn. Now combined with commentary on 1 & 2 Thessalonians (previously unpublished), this volume of the *PBC* series shows Paul's characteristic energy and passion as he writes to the new churches.

1 THESSALONIANS 1:6, 7

The REVOLUTION of FAITH

Paul continues to remind his readers in Thessalonica of what happened when he and his two companions preached the gospel there. The result of the preaching was evidence of God's approval of the believers; God had worked a miracle in the lives of the Thessalonians by changing their minds and this had become known to others in that part of the world.

Paul's argument is still that faith is strengthened by reflecting on experience; what happened to us is best explained as the action of God.

The particular point made here is that though the believers became the object of other people's hatred, though they were persecuted, they were nevertheless filled with joy. Suffering co-existed with joy. In most circumstances we would expect ill-treatment to produce sadness and misery; the normal person wants to be popular, and resents and avoids scorn. But it was not so when the gospel was preached in Thessalonica; the Holy Spirit imparted joy to those who believed the good news, even when they were being ill-used by others.

Paul and his companions had been maltreated in Philippi, when they were on the way to Thessalonica (see 1 Thessalonians 2:1, 2), so the Thessalonians knew what to expect. Then they found themselves in the same situation. Both

20

they and those who preached to them were following the pattern of the Lord himself. The preaching concerned Christ crucified, and it was the opposite of everyday wisdom which said that in order to be joyful you must be comfortable and success- *Rejoice* ful. Paul will say later that the gospel is the word of *always!* God, not a human word (1 Thessalonians 2:13): it tells us things that we would not otherwise know. One of these things is that it is possible (necessary, in fact) to be joyful on all occasions and in all circumstances. Paul will say so, explicitly, at the end of this letter: 'Rejoice always' (1 Thessalonians 5:16).

Finding joy

The gospel contradicts worldly wisdom. It involves the story of someone who failed to persuade others to follow him, was isolated from his friends, died in darkness and disgrace, mocked to death by the authorities, and who thought himself abandoned by God who had turned his face against him (see Mark 15). This is the saving event, the way in which God acts in the world. It teaches us to disconnect the search for joy from what we imagine to be self-fulfilment, but to find it instead in what destroys our plans and frustrates our hopes and expectations. What we thought impossible—joy, and the annihilation of self-will—turns out not to be so; blessedness is to be found in having nothing.

The faith that can accept this stands out in an otherwise drab and worldly world of pleasure-seeking and competitiveness. It is so unusual that it cannot go unnoticed. All over Macedonia and Achaia, other believers have heard about the joy of the persecuted Thessalonians, and been encouraged by it. The faith of one church is strengthened by hearing about the faith of another. Faith feeds on faith and is nourished by it.

Paul had used the expression earlier, '…your work of faith' (1:3), and this may be an example of what faith does. It works by turning things into their opposites. (Paul will give a list of them in 2 Corinthians 6:8–10.) What we had most feared, and thus tried to avoid, becomes what we prize most highly; what we had dreaded is welcomed; what we had hoped to escape is accepted. Faith turns minuses into pluses, and pluses into minuses. The first are last, and the last first.

PRAYER

*Give me faith to see everything in reverse:
to accept what I now resist;
to want to be nothing myself, but you to be everything.*

The next four PBC commentaries will be published in February 2001.

Profile—
Mark Greene

According to research conducted by Mark Greene while he was based at London Bible College (LBC), 47 per cent of people in evangelical churches said that the sermons they heard each week were actually irrelevant to their daily lives. As far as issues of personal spirituality and to some extent church life were concerned, teaching was felt to be 'not bad', but when it came to connecting with the everyday world of work, most people received the strong impression that the Bible had nothing helpful to say.

Mark's research also found that fifty per cent of people had never heard a sermon on work, although their ministers would regularly preach through different parts of the Bible:

A minister might preach on Genesis and take an angle that involved dealing with questions of science, racism, even chauvinism, but never think to mention that God is actually seen as a worker. Or they might read the Psalms and never see that the people opposing David sound exactly like the criticism found in competitive corporate atmospheres today. We need what I call 11 o'clock theology—an approach which takes account of where we are at 11am on a Monday morning. We need to help people live as Christians where they are throughout the week, not just on Sundays.

Mark is former Vice Principal of LBC and he also lectured there in Communication, the Bible and Contemporary Culture. Since 1999, however, he has been Executive Director of the London Institute for Contemporary Christianity (LICC). The Institute was originally set up in 1982 by John Stott of All Souls, Langham Place, in London, with the aim of helping Christians both in Britain and abroad to engage biblically with the many issues that they face in daily life. The idea of such an institute emerged as John Stott realized that the contemporary criticism of Christianity was not that it was untrue, but that it was irrelevant.

This desire to make Christianity relevant finds expression in Mark's passion for equipping people to communicate their faith clearly to those with whom they are in daily contact, as well as teaching intelligent use of the Bible in dealing with every aspect of culture:

> *Christian youthwork, for example, has tended to be focused on sex, drugs and rock 'n' roll, with advice being 'wait, no, and it depends'— and you have to make sure that you get the order right! Churches have not equipped young people to think biblically about what they are actually studying at school, whether it's Hamlet or geography.*

One example Mark cites is developing a theology of mathematics—something that everybody has to study at school but which few try to 'think Christianly' about. In fact, profound insights can be found embedded within mathematical structures: $1+1+1=3$ may not help us understand the Trinity, but how about $1 \times 1 \times 1 = 1$?

The Institute has perhaps had its most significant impact overseas, through the annual ten-week 'Christian in the Modern World' course, which more than 500 have attended since its conception seventeen years ago. Around twenty Institutes have sprung up around the world, modelled on the London centre, and Christians returning from the course to their home countries have moved into positions of church leadership, influencing and challenging Christian witness within their own cultures. In the UK, many people have been trained through Christian Impact Weekends, run by LICC throughout the country. London Christians, meanwhile, have benefited from courses and one-off seminars provided at the Institute's headquarters at St Peter's Church, Vere Street.

This ministry to Christians living in and around London is set to continue and strengthen, but for the future Mark stresses the need to develop LICC as a specialist resource for Christians in the marketplace, for students in Bible and theological colleges and for Christian leaders. Unfortunately, the majority of UK Bible colleges simply don't yet have the staff or resources to provide sufficient training in communication skills or in relating biblical faith to today's culture. This lack of training has led to many UK Christians feeling ill-equipped either to share the basics of their faith or to relate their beliefs to the world around them. Through LICC, Mark is developing a team of people who can address Christian leaders, college students, and Christians in general, and help them tackle some of the many issues that clamour for attention. A focus on these issues—to do with the workplace, media, youth culture, the role of women, capitalism, pluralism—is combined with learning the communication skills necessary to connect with friends, neighbours, colleagues and, not least, church members! This will all be facilitated by conferences, provision of resource materials (video and print), and training courses.

Mark himself fully appreciates the tension between Christian faith and the world of work, as he spent ten years working at the advertising agency Ogilvy and Mather, first in London and then in New York. Originally from a Jewish background, he became a Christian at the age of 23 and took three years to start going to church, finally joining a Baptist congregation in New York. Returning to the UK, he went to study at LBC, in North London, and ended up on the teaching staff there. Somebody who influenced him greatly during his time there was Peter Cotterell, who later retired from being Principal of the college and went to Ethiopia to start a graduate school:

I found him an extraordinary man of God. As a manager, he could take all the decisions he had to take as Principal, while still giving you the feeling that you had been listened to in the process, even if he didn't do what you advised. And he was very good at understanding different cultural groups, able to relate to people much younger than himself without feeling he had to put on a pair of jeans to do so!

Mark still lives near LBC, with his Finnish wife Katriina and their three children—Matti (8), Tomas (5), and Anna-Marie (3). Besides his lecturing work, he has written a number of books: *Opening Night* (poetry, Lion), *Thank God It's Monday* (workplace issues, SU), and *Of Love, Life and Caffe Latte* (Azure), a book offering biblical perspectives on a range of contemporary issues in a style accessible to both Christians and non-Christians alike.

Working in his office in an adapted church, he looks out each day at its illustrious East Window, designed by Burne-Jones, which depicts the meeting of Jesus and the woman at the well (John 4). Although the stained-glass scene is inevitably stylized with a blonde-haired Jesus, Mark finds it curiously inspiring:

It stands above the altar and the cross, and is a startling reminder of how Jesus communicated with people outside his culture. The woman is at work, drawing her water, and Jesus is reaching out to her—one of a race despised by the Jews—the Samaritans—five times married and involved with a man she's not married to… There is a risk in engaging with people from 'outside'—those around you may disapprove—but, like Jesus, we too have to reach out.

For further information about LICC, contact St Peter's Church, Vere St, London W1M 9HP.
Tel: 0207-3999 555
E-mail mail@licc.org.uk

Joshua

Nations and civilizations are born, and nations and civilizations die. Stories of new beginnings and the conquest of new lands form part of the traditional culture and history of many peoples.

Yet nations are scarcely ever formed in isolation by occupying 'virgin territory'. So the inhabitants of late Roman Britain are displaced by the Anglo-Saxons, pushed into the west of the islands, the 'Celtic fringe'. In Central and South America and the Caribbean, the civilizations of the Aztecs, Incas and Caribs are swept away. In the nineteenth century, the North American Indians are in retreat and the lands of Australia, New Zealand and South Africa are not empty of peoples when European settlers arrive. Returning Jews create the State of Israel in 1948, but this results in the awful problem of the displacement of Palestinians.

These examples from history perhaps help to put the book of Joshua in perspective. The exploits of the generation that first took possession of the Promised Land are extolled in this book. Joshua is undoubtedly a book of propaganda. It is hardly surprising, therefore, that while modern Israelis rejoice in its contents, modern Palestinians find it almost impossible to read. Their sympathies are more likely to be with the Canaanite tribes than with Joshua's aggressive invaders.

The events portrayed in the book of Joshua are generally dated in the period 1250 to 1200BC, though some scholars place them at least two hundred years earlier. No doubt the exploits were told by storytellers and singers long before they were written down. The final form of the book that we now have in our Bibles comes from a much later period. It is part of the lengthy history work that includes all of Joshua, Judges, Samuel and Kings. Scholars often refer to these books as the 'Deuteronomistic History' since they continue the theology and outlook of Deuteronomy.

So as we read these gripping but often highly disturbing tales, let us try to see them as part of the 'big picture', as part of the biblical story of salvation. We may need to penetrate behind the rhetoric and propaganda to discover what God might be saying to us today, especially in the area of 'new beginnings'.

1   **A new leader**   *Read Joshua 1:1–18*

The book of Joshua marks a new beginning, and a completely new
section of the Bible. In the Hebrew Bible, the close of Deuteronomy marks the end of the Law (Torah). Joshua signifies the
beginning of the history books of Joshua to 2 Kings. One age has
passed—the age of the wilderness wanderings—and a new age is
about to dawn—the age of conquest and settlement.

None the less, the author of the book of Joshua is keen to stress
the sense of continuity. Joshua has been groomed for this moment,
and the first lieutenant now takes over the reins of command. There
is a smooth transition between the 'age of Moses' and the 'age of
Joshua'. The promise made to Moses is confirmed (v. 3) and Joshua
is assured, 'As I was with Moses, so I will be with you' (v. 5).

The promises of God, however, demand a human response. No
less than four times, in verses 6, 7, 9 and 18, Joshua is encouraged
to 'be strong and very courageous'. Linked to that command is the
requirement to be faithful to 'this book of the law' (v. 8). It may be
that the reference is to the laws in the central section of
Deuteronomy (chapters 12—26). The words are addressed, of
course, not just to Joshua and his generation but to all succeeding
generations too.

Verses 10–11 describe the need for food supplies to be prepared
for the campaign that lies ahead. The need to get provisions in this
way may be an indication that the God-given supply of manna is
about to come to an end. The wilderness wanderings are no more.
A new era is about to begin for the people here on the border of
the land 'flowing with milk and honey'.

Verses 12–18 speak of the two and one-half tribes that were
settled east of the Jordan. There is a need for solidarity at this
point. The tribes of Reuben, Gad and the eastern half of the tribe
of Manasseh were already in possession of their tribal allotment.
They could have opted to stay on the far side of the Jordan River
and let the other tribes fight for their own lands. The leaders
answer Joshua positively. They will obey Joshua as they did Moses
(v. 17) and they exhort him to be strong and courageous (v. 18).
In this case, 'unity is strength'.

2   Spying out the land   *Read Joshua 2:1–16*

The site of the city of Jericho is one of the most important in the Jordan valley. It is often described as one of the oldest inhabited cities in the world, with evidence of early occupation going back to 7000 or 8000BC. It is a fertile oasis, a city of palm trees towards the southern end of the River Jordan before it enters the Dead Sea. It would be an important strategic city for Joshua and his army to capture at the beginning of their campaign.

The spies who are sent out find an unlikely ally in the person of Rahab. What led her to throw in her lot with the enemy forces? The reason given in verses 9–11 is a theological one. Rahab makes a confession of faith in the Lord, the God of Israel. She rehearses the great things that the Lord has done and how they have left the inhabitants of Jericho dispirited and fearful. A cynic might say that she saw the way the wind was blowing and joined the winning side! Others might conclude that she was hedging her bets, or perhaps seeking a better life than she had as a prostitute in the Canaanite environment of Jericho. Of these mean reasons the biblical text knows nothing. Rahab becomes, in effect, a convert to the Israelite faith.

As a woman of 'ill repute', Rahab receives a surprising number of mentions in the New Testament. The genealogy list in Matthew 1:5 identifies her as the wife of Salman and mother of Boaz, the hero of the story of Ruth. Thus she is an ancestress both of David and of Jesus himself. The letter to the Hebrews (11:31) and the epistle of James (2:25) both praise her for her actions, the former for her faith and the latter for her deeds. Thus a character who might easily be condemned because of her way of life and betrayal of her own people becomes a symbol of conversion. She enters into a covenant pact with the people of God and thereby saves herself and her whole household.

3   'The verge of Jordan'   *Read Joshua 3:1–17*

The moment has finally come for the Israelites to set foot in the promised land. Their ancestor Abraham had wandered this land with his herds and flocks. Jacob and his family had abandoned the land of promise. It had become a land of famine, and Egypt was their place of safety. Now the infant nation of the children of Israel stands on the very edge of the land. Only the boundary of the Jordan River separates them from the land of milk and honey.

This is indeed a moment for crossing boundaries. As the ark, the symbol of the presence of God, has led them through the wilderness, so now it goes before them into the promised future. The miracle of the Jordan crossing is a deliberate echo of the miracle at the Red Sea. There too, walls of water piled up on either side (Exodus 14:22—15:8). So as they entered the wilderness and freedom through the waters, so now they leave the wilderness and enter into their inheritance. This is a very significant boundary to cross.

For Christians, the imagery of crossing the Jordan is inevitably linked with baptism. Furthermore, the traditional site of Jesus' baptism in the Jordan is not far from the spot opposite Jericho where this miracle is located. The image of 'crossing the Jordan' has become a very powerful one in Christian literature and song. It is at its most powerful in Bunyan's *Pilgrim's Progress* where the end of the pilgrim's life is depicted as crossing over the Jordan: 'So he passed over, and all the trumpets sounded for him on the other side'. Christian hymnwriters too have made much of the image.

> *When I tread the verge of Jordan*
> *Bid my anxious fears subside*
> *Death of death and hell's destruction*
> *Land me safe on Canaan's side.*

> William Williams (1717–91)

4   Memorial stones   *Read Joshua 4:1–20*

The story of the crossing of the Jordan continues with a fuller description of the events. The importance of the number twelve is stressed—twelve tribes and twelve marker stones, emphasizing that all Israel is involved. Perhaps the twelve stands in deliberate opposition to the seven Canaanite tribes listed in 3:10.

The main emphasis in this chapter, however, is on the importance of memory. Passing on the traditions to succeeding generations is a very significant motif in the book of Deuteronomy (see Deuteronomy 6). The book of Joshua continues the same theme, the crucial significance of memory. The stories told in the book of Joshua are not there simply for entertainment. They are there to ensure the continuation of the national memory.

The stones themselves also play their part. In a similar fashion, national monuments or village war memorials do the same for us today. The narrative seems to envisage two sets of stones. Most attention is paid to the twelve stones set up on the west bank of the Jordan, near Gilgal (v. 20). However, verse 9 also mentions twelve stones placed in the River Jordan. Perhaps these indicated the site of an ancient ford and were visible when the river was running low.

Verse 19 mentions the date of these events, and a significant date too in the Hebrew calendar. The tenth day of the first month was the day on which the Passover lambs were chosen (Exodus 12:3). So it is springtime, when the Jordan runs high (see 3:15) with meltwater from the snows of Mount Hermon in the north. Perhaps each spring the tribes would gather at the shrine at Gilgal especially to remember the events of the first crossing of the Jordan. The sanctuary at Gilgal is portrayed as the first Israelite settlement in the promised land, and it is mentioned on a number of occasions later in the Old Testament as an important shrine for early Israel's worship. It was the place, for instance, where Saul was crowned as first king of Israel (1 Samuel 11:14–15).

5   Before the battle   *Read Joshua 5:1–15*

Of the seven nations occupying the promised land, two were most prominent, the Amorites in the central hill country and the Canaanites down in the coastal plain. Sometimes these names can be used for the whole of the pre-Israelite population.

The story told in verses 1–9 explains the names of two places, a common feature of Hebrew storytelling. A hill near Gilgal was given the name Gibeath-haaraloth, or Hill of Foreskins, to commemorate this event. The name Gilgal itself is linked to the Hebrew verb 'to roll away'. God has now rolled away the disgrace of the people (v. 9). They are no longer humiliated slaves but a free people about to take possession of the land.

Many of the wilderness generation had not been circumcised, and so this is remedied. Again it points to the new beginning for this generation. According to Exodus 12:48, only those who had been circumcised could eat the Passover. So this chapter goes on to describe the first Passover in the land, celebrated on the fourteenth day of the month. Passover is a spring festival at the time of the barley harvest. Now that the Israelites have entered the promised land, the supply of miraculous food, the manna, comes to an end. The nomads must become farmers and grow their own produce. They will have to learn that the God of the wilderness also provides the rains that water the land so that it will yield its crops.

Finally, in verses 13–15, there is a brief description of Joshua's encounter with the angel of the Lord. There are echoes of similar encounters in other parts of the Bible. When Jacob was returning to Canaan, he too met a mysterious stranger by the fords of Jabbok (Genesis 32). The angel of the Lord would appear also to characters such as Gideon (Judges 6). The instruction to Joshua to take off his sandals because the place is holy is a deliberate echo of the story of Moses at the burning bush (Exodus 3). Once more Joshua is portrayed as the legitimate successor to Moses.

Joshua wants to know which side the angel is on—for 'us' or for 'them'—but the angel refuses to be conscripted in such a way. In the New Testament, James and John wanted to identify clearly those who were among the 'in group', and were rebuked by Jesus (Mark 10:38–39). Every religious tradition likes to feel that it has God on its side. The point of this story is that God cannot be so easily manipulated. Despite appearance, the God of the book of Joshua is not merely a national or tribal deity. God is sovereign and will act with sovereign freedom, which can be disturbing and disconcerting to our tidy minds and systems.

6 Tumbling down *Read Joshua 6:1–3, 12–27*

'Joshua fought the battle of Jericho, and the walls came a-tumbling down,' according to the song. It is indeed a dramatic picture, but how close is it to historical reality? The ruins of the ancient Bronze Age Canaanite city of Jericho are usually identified with the mound called Tel es Sultan. A great deal of excavation has been done in there, but the results are inconclusive. In the 1930s, the archaeologist John Garstang thought he could identify, among the debris, walls from the time of Joshua in the late Bronze Age. In the 1950s, new findings by Dame Kathleen Kenyon suggested that these walls were actually much older, and that Jericho was already a ruin by the late Bronze Age. We need to remember that what the archaeologist uncovers always needs to be interpreted, just like a biblical text, and different interpretations are possible. Archaeology can never really 'prove' or 'disprove' the biblical account.

Perhaps, rather than searching for historical clues, we should concentrate instead on the theological dimension of the story. The procession round the walls has all the hallmarks of a religious procession, with priests, ark and trumpets. Reference to the 'great shout' and 'trumpet blast' echoes the language of liturgical celebration. It is in this context that we should understand the spoils of war being 'entirely devoted' to God, and not used for personal gain.

Special mention is made of Rahab and her family. This Canaanite group continued to live in the Jericho area (v. 25). Sometimes the book of Joshua gives the impression of a wholesale slaughter of all Canaanites, the Old Testament equivalent of ethnic cleansing. The reality was almost certainly far more complicated than that. This mention of Rahab, along with other hints in Joshua and Judges, suggests that there continued to be many non-Israelites living within the borders of the promised land.

The whole site of Jericho was 'put under the ban' and remained a ruin for hundreds of years. This is despite the fact that there are many springs in the area which would make it an ideal place for settlement. The curse on the site is pronounced in verse 26. The story is told in 1 Kings 16:34 of how, in the time of King Ahab in the ninth century, a man called Hiel finally rebuilt the city, but at great personal cost.

GUIDELINES

The events of the thirteenth century BC may seem remote and far away. Yet many of the issues that these stories raise can be easily translated into our present day. As you look back on Joshua 1—6, consider how aspects of these national events can shed light on your own personal story. See if you can remember any of the following:

- *A time when you had to 'be strong and courageous' (ch. 1).*

- *An occasion when you found unexpected allies in a cause that meant much to you (ch. 2).*

- *A significant moment of change or transition in your life—the crossing of a boundary (ch. 3).*

- *The places or events that are your own personal 'memorial stones' (ch. 4).*

- *A moment of encounter that made you reassess your picture of God (ch. 5).*

- *Any time when you have had to do battle with hostile forces (ch. 6).*

Be still, recollect, and offer these times back to God.

11–17 SEPTEMBER   JOSHUA 7:1—14:15

1   'Sins of the fathers'   *Read Joshua 7:1–5, 16–26*

For modern readers, the story in Joshua 7 is one of the most disturbing in the Bible. As a result of Achan's sin, not only he himself but his whole family bear the punishment (v. 15). Our modern sensibilities are deeply offended by this and we are likely to condemn the chapter as barbaric. Yet we need to try to understand the thinking behind the chapter—even if we do not agree with it.

    The sin of Achan is to break the rules concerning the 'ban'. He takes for himself some of the devoted things which should have been handed over for sacred use. He seeks to make personal gain and buries the objects in his own tent (v. 21). Achan's 'little private sin' turns out to have very public consequences. The attempt to capture the city of Ai ends in defeat and humiliation for the Israelites. On the face of it, it would seem that they were just over-confident (vv. 2–5) about how easy it would be to take Ai after the success at Jericho. However, the reason for the defeat is put down to sin on the part of Israel (v. 11). By a process of elimination, the household of Achan is gradually singled out (vv. 17–18).

In the West, we tend to see everything in very individual terms, but this way of thinking was alien to the biblical writers. They shared a belief in what is often called 'corporate personality'. It is well summed up in the phrase from the Ten Commandments about 'visiting the iniquity of the fathers upon the children unto the third and fourth generation' (Exodus 20:5, KJV). The sins that individuals commit have wide repercussions, far beyond the individuals themselves. In this respect, the Hebrews were right: sin does not stop at the individual level. Rather, it has a corrupting effect on all those around it. Achan can hardly have hidden his ill-gotten gains without some of his close family knowing about it. Thus the whole family is implicated and corrupted. We modern readers may be offended by the story, but we need to relearn the truth about the corrupting effect of evil on the life of a community.

A cairn of stones is built to mark the spot and the place receives a memorial name—the Valley of Achor, or 'Trouble Valley' (v. 26). It is a desolate spot located up above the site of Qumran, near where the Dead Sea Scrolls were found. Yet even this desolate place could be transformed in the imagination of the prophets. Hosea looks forward to a time when God will 'make the Valley of Achor a door of hope' (Hosea 2:15).

2   A trick with mouldy bread   Read Joshua 9:1–15

The death of Achan at the end of chapter 7 is followed in chapter 8 by the successful conquest of the city of Ai. Joshua and his forces are now in control of much of the southern area of the Jordan Valley. They are ready for the next stage of military advance which will take them up into the central hill country near Jerusalem.

The town of Gibeon is situated about six miles north-west of Jerusalem. The city, along with three other settlements (v. 17), was occupied by the people known as the Hivites (v. 7), one of the groups that occupied Canaan before the Israelite conquest (v. 2). Like the prostitute Rahab in chapter 2, the Gibeonites decide to 'defect' to the Israelite side. However, it is one thing to accept a family into the nation, but quite another to incorporate a whole town into Israel. Therefore the Gibeonites decide on a crafty trick, and the author takes some delight in spelling out the details. The depiction of the mouldy bread, patched wineskins and worn-out clothing is a wonderful piece of storytelling.

In verse 14 we are told that 'the leaders partook of the provisions'. Although not absolutely clear, this probably means that the Israelite leaders shared in the unappetizing provisions of the Gibeonites. The whole point of this is that by sharing food together the two groups become bound to one another. There are a number of instances in the Bible where a covenant treaty is sealed by a shared meal. In the ancient world, once you had shared table fellowship together you were bound into a relationship with the other.

So, in modern slang, the Gibeonites have 'pulled a fast one'! They have deceived the unsuspecting Israelites. The author comments in verse 15 that the leaders were at fault. They took too much upon themselves and did not consult the Lord in this matter.

3 'Hewers of wood'   *Read Joshua 9:16–27*

Once a covenant promise had been made and an oath sworn, it was impossible to go back on it, even if it had been obtained with trickery. This is the lesson of the story of Jacob, Esau and the deception of the old, blind Isaac in Genesis 27. Jacob receives his father's blessing by trickery, but the blessing cannot be taken away. Now, ironically, the descendants of Jacob, the Israelites, find themselves tricked.

Consequently the Gibeonites can no longer be treated like the rest of the Canaanite tribes. Nor can they simply be incorporated into the twelve-tribe alliance of the sons of Jacob. They therefore occupy an ambiguous status in Israel. They are allowed to remain in the land, but they are not to have full citizen rights. The phrase used in this chapter is that they become 'hewers of wood and drawers of water'. In other words, they are to do the menial tasks and are not to be in any position of prominence—not a very appealing picture, and one that echoes elements of the caste system in India. Perhaps, though, we should be asking who are the equivalents to these 'hewers of wood and drawers of water' in our own society. Are there social or ethnic groups that are consistently pushed to the bottom of the socio-economic system? Until we face up to that reality in our own societies, will we be in any position to judge the ancient Israelites? Remember, Jesus spoke about removing the 'beams' from our own eyes before seeking to remove the 'specks' from others'.

The work the Gibeonites do is 'for the congregation and for the altar' (v. 27). So their tasks were linked to the sanctuary, probably the local sanctuary at Gibeon at first, and then later at the temple in Jerusalem. Perhaps in due time the Gibeonites became loyal worshippers of the Lord, with an accepted place even in the courts of the Lord's house. Clearly the author of the book of Joshua knows full well that the 'conquest' of Canaan was not complete. For a long time there remained a body of non-Israelites within the population and this story explains one reason why this should be, even down to the writer's own day.

4   Strategy and miracle   *Read Joshua 10:1–15*

Recent events have caused panic among the rulers of the city states of Canaan. The forces of Joshua represent a new and different culture to the old, decaying cities of late Bronze Age Canaan. The king of Jerusalem therefore forms a coalition with four other kings, whose cities lie to the south and east. They include the city of Hebron, near where the bones of Abraham and Sarah lie in the cave at Machpelah (Genesis 25).

The people of Gibeon call upon their new allies for help, and the Israelites show their covenant loyalty by responding to the plea. This battle will be of great importance strategically. If they can win it, the Israelites will take control of a whole swathe of countryside in the southern and central hill-country—the area that was eventually occupied by the tribes of Judah and Benjamin.

Victory in the battle comes about as a result of good strategic planning on the part of Joshua (v. 9), combined with help from the Lord God (v. 10). Celestial wonders accompany the battle—stones from heaven and the standing still of sun and moon (vv. 11–14). There are two standard responses from commentators to these remarkable events:

- *the naturalist response, which seeks to give a 'rational' explanation in terms of hailstones, thunder, clouds, etc.*

- *the supernaturalist response, which accepts the story at face value as the action of an interventionist God.*

These two responses cannot really be reconciled and I suspect that readers of *Guidelines* can be found in both camps! The author himself seems to set out to show that, ultimately, victory belongs to the Lord and not to human effort (for example, more are killed by hailstones than by the sword). God is Lord of creation and momentous events are appropriately marked by remarkable signs in the heavens. In the same way, the Gospel writers speak of three hours of darkness at the time of the crucifixion of Jesus (Matthew 27:45).

Finally, reference is made to the account of this battle given in the Book of Jashar. This work is now lost to us, but is referred to again in 2 Samuel 1:18. Presumably it was one of the sources which the compiler of Joshua and the other history books used in helping to write the 'deuteronomistic history' of Joshua to 2 Kings.

5   A new society   *Read Joshua 13:1–14*

Having conquered first the Jordan valley and then the central hill-country, the army of Joshua goes on to defeat the northern coalition of kings, led by the king of Hazor. This story is told in chapter 11, with a comment in 11:23 that after that 'the land had rest from war'. Chapter 12 contains a list of all the kings defeated by Joshua's invaders. So by the end of chapter 12, the halfway point of the book of Joshua, the enemies have been subdued.

However, destruction needs to be followed by construction, and the rest of the book of Joshua is concerned with the building up of a new society to replace the corrupt society of Canaan. The next main section of the book, chapters 13—22, tells in great detail the exact boundaries of each of the twelve tribes. The material largely consists of the names of towns and villages, and does not make for exciting reading, like reading a gazetteer or a list of names from an Ordnance Survey map. Yet even such unpromising material is of great interest to ancient historians. Without these lists, it would be impossible to construct the maps we find today in Bible atlases or at the end of our Bibles.

The distribution of the land takes place while Joshua is still alive (v. 1). This is despite the fact that, for all the famous victories, parts of the promised land are still in the possession of other nations. Attention is drawn first to the southern coastal plain, where the newly arrived Philistines occupy their five cities (vv. 2–3). There are also areas of non-Israelite settlement in the north, around Sidon (v. 4) and towards the Lebanon (vv. 5–6).

Verses 8–13 outline the general area occupied by the two and a half tribes that settled east of the Jordan. The rest of the chapter goes on to give more specific details of the land holdings of the three tribes of Reuben, Gad and East Manasseh. Once more, pockets of non-Israelite population are mentioned, especially around Maacath and Gesher. (This northern Gesher is different from the southern one mentioned in verse 2.) Finally, verse 14 comments briefly on the fact that the tribe of Levi owned no land. Special provision was made for this priestly tribe. This was all part of the arrangements for a new society outlined in the book of Joshua. 'Canaan' became 'Israel' and the hierarchical city states were replaced by a more radical and revolutionary vision of equality and responsibility.

6   Caleb and his clan   *Read Joshua 14:1–15*

The land of the two and a half tribes east of the Jordan was described in chapter 13. With chapter 14, attention moves to the nine and a half tribes west of the Jordan. Chapters 15—19 will go into great detail concerning the specific boundaries, towns and villages of each tribe. Chapter 14 itself includes an introduction in verses 1–5 and a story about Caleb and the city of Hebron in verses 6–15.

Verse 2 mentions that allocation of the land was by lot. This was a sacred means of deciding the will of God—hence in Acts 1:26 the apostles cast lots to decide who should take the place of Judas Iscariot, 'and the lot fell on Matthias'. In Old Testament times, the high priest kept in his breastplate the sacred lots called Urim and Thummim (Exodus 28:30). It is not surprising, therefore, to find the priest Eleazar mentioned alongside Joshua in the casting of these lots. Eleazar was the son and heir of Aaron, the high priest. In the wilderness, the duo of Moses and Aaron led the people. Now in the promised land their rightful successors, Joshua and Eleazar, occupy the same leadership roles. Attention is again drawn to the fact that Levi has no land of its own. If you remove Levi from the twelve tribes, you are left with only eleven. However, the tribe of Joseph was allocated two portions, one for each of his two sons, Ephraim and Manasseh (Genesis 48). Hence Bible atlases showing the twelve tribal lands will not include Levi or Joseph but Ephraim and Manasseh instead.

Caleb was one of the spies sent by Moses to do a reconnaissance of the promised land (Numbers 13—14). Only he and Joshua brought back a favourable report. The rest of the spies were afraid of the fearsome Anakim and their strong fortifications. Consequently only Joshua and Caleb are permitted to enter the promised land; the rest of their generation dies out. Now the old soldier finally prepares to settle down and chooses the area around the southern city of Hebron, formerly known as Kiriath-arba (v. 15). Clearly the Caleb clan formed an important enclave within the tribal territory of Judah (15:13–19). Caleb is described as being a Kenizzite in 14:14. This name may be taken from that of his brother, Kenaz, mentioned in 15:17. However, it is possible that originally the Kenizzites were a group independent of the Israelites. In Genesis 36:11 they are among the original inhabitants of Canaan, and according to Genesis 36:11 and 42 they had links with the family of Esau. So possibly this story explains how this group came to occupy the land around Hebron, though here in Joshua 14 Caleb is portrayed as a full member of the people of Israel. Some scholars think that the Caleb group may have occupied the promised land from the south, while the Joshua group came across the Jordan from the east.

GUIDELINES

This week's readings have depicted bloody battles, treaty alliances and the creation of a new society to replace the old order. It is a story of both success and failure—of great victories and of land that remained out of reach. It is a story of both ruthlessness and compromise—contrast the fate of most of the Canaanite inhabitants with that of the tricky Gibeonites. It has its villains (Achan) and its heroes (Caleb). Into the turbulent scene tumble all kinds of people, all sorts of emotions.

The Bible can be a disturbing book as well as a challenging one. It nevertheless has the power to open windows on our own situations, both personal and corporate. As you reflect on the readings this week, try to make connections with your own situation.

- *Consider the mixture of success and failure in your own life, and how you have dealt with it.*

- *Recall those times when you have determinedly stood out for what you believed right, and those times when you knew you had to make compromises.*

- *Bring to mind the heroes and heroines who have inspired you in your Christian journey and the battles that had to be fought.*

18–24 SEPTEMBER   JOSHUA 20:1—24:33

1   Cities set apart   *Read Joshua 20:1–9; 21:1–8*

Chapters 13—19 of Joshua give details of each of the tribal lands. The next two chapters deal with cities 'set apart' for particular purposes. Chapter 20 describes the system of 'cities of refuge' for asylum seekers, while chapter 21 outlines the 'levitical cities' where members of the tribe of Levi could live.

The need for cities of refuge is mentioned twice in the Law of Moses (Numbers 35 and Deuteronomy 19). They were to form an essential part of the system for the administration of justice in the land. The judicial system was still in a very early form and responsibility for obtaining justice and recompense largely fell on the family that had been affected, especially when a family member had been killed. Family honour was, and still is, of great concern in many societies. It was the responsibility of the next of kin to put things right by slaying the one who had shed innocent blood. But what should happen where there had been an accidental killing? One revenge killing could lead to another, and the land become utterly polluted by the shedding of blood. So the system of six cities of refuge, three on each side of the Jordan, was devised.

The idea of sanctuary persisted into medieval times in Europe, where the great cathedrals were often seen as places of sanctuary. In modern times, some churches in Britain and elsewhere have been used by those seeking sanctuary. Note how the death of the high priest releases the asylum seekers (20:6). It is as though his death brings an end to the contamination of the land; as though he somehow carries the sin. Christians will readily see a parallel between the death of Jesus 'for our sakes' and that of the priest.

Chapter 21 gives details of the 48 cities set aside for the Levites, which include the six cities of refuge (Numbers 35:6). Verses 4–7 refer to four levitical groups. The line of Kohath was the one from which Aaron was descended and is therefore divided between those who were priests (the descendants of Aaron) and those who were not ('ordinary' Levites, not of Aaron's line). The full details of all 48 levitical cities are given in verses 9–45.

2   Unity threatened   *Read Joshua 22:1–20*

The author of the book of Joshua is always keen to stress the unity of the twelve-tribe coalition under Joshua. 'All for one and one for all' was the motto. Right at the beginning, in chapter 1, the tribes of Reuben, Gad and East Manasseh were exhorted to fight alongside their brothers (1:12–15). To this they readily agreed (1:16–18) and left behind their families in order to conquer the land of Canaan.

Verses 1–9 recount how they have faithfully kept their word and shown real solidarity with the tribes of the west (v. 3). Verse 7 mentions in passing the division of the tribe of Manasseh into two parts, West and East. East Manasseh occupies the land of Bashan beyond the Sea of Galilee. The tribes part on good terms at the sanctuary at Shiloh (v. 9). From the time of Joshua, the ark of the covenant resided here (18:1) and it remained a very important sanctuary for a long time. It was at Shiloh that the young boy Samuel was to minister before the Lord (1 Samuel 1).

However, the unity of the tribes is threatened by what happens next. Somewhere near the fords of the Jordan, the easterners build a large altar. Exactly where is not certain, as the Hebrew of verses 10–11 is not clear. The NRSV translation situates it on the west side, whereas the Jerusalem Bible has it on the east. The real problem is not its exact location but what this altar represents. Any altar built without the express command of God was potentially dangerous. It could become a focus for false worship and idolatrous practices.

Phineas, the son of Eleazar and grandson of Aaron, is sent with a delegation to investigate. Phineas is a deliberate choice, since he is a fervent follower of the Lord. Verse 17 mentions the 'sin at Peor'. This incident of idolatry is described in Numbers 25 and it was this same Phineas who put a stop to it. The delegation questions the easterners and asks them whether they think their land is polluted, and whether that is why they built the altar. This may betray a sense of superiority on the part of the westerners. Perhaps they believe that they occupy the 'real' promised land, and that the land of Gilead (v. 9) on the east is decidedly inferior. It is a tense moment and the threat of war hangs in the air. The unity of all Israel seems to be on the brink of total collapse.

3 Unity restored *Read Joshua 22:21–34*

The tension is at its height, and the threat of civil war is very real. Such intertribal conflict could indeed break out, as the story of the punishment of the tribe of Benjamin portrays (Judges 20).

The eastern tribes affirm clearly and unequivocally their loyalty to the Lord, the covenant God of Israel. The altar is not meant to be a rival shrine to the one set up at Shiloh. Rather, it is to be a tangible symbol, a 'visual aid' to both east and west.

The Jordan River was a significant boundary between the west and the east, between 'Israel proper' and the lands of Transjordan. There is, therefore, a real fear expressed that, in time to come, east and west will go their separate ways. Those living in 'Israel proper' might come to reject the claim of the eastern tribes to belong to the true Israel. The emphasis in these verses is particularly on the two tribes of Reuben and Gad. They occupied the plateau overlooking the Jordan valley between the Dead Sea and the Sea of Galilee. They were perhaps right to be concerned, for they were near neighbours of the Moabites, Ammonites and the Aramean tribes of Syria. As such, their land was vulnerable to invasion and they themselves to a loss of identity.

The altar therefore stands not as an alternative, rival shrine. It is not even for offering sacrifice. Rather it stands as a witness between the tribes (v. 34), a witness to their common ancestry and brotherly commitment. Having heard the explanation, Phineas and his company are satisfied and return to their homes. Warfare is averted and the bond of unity is preserved.

This story reminds us that nationalities and groups can and do drift apart. Those who were once friends can become enemies. The easterners had good reason to be concerned. The tribe of Reuben soon disappeared from history, even though he was the eldest son of Jacob/Israel, and the eastern tribes were eventually overwhelmed by their neighbours and by the might of Assyria. Perhaps this story was retained by the final editor of the book for a reason. Writing perhaps in the seventh century BC, in the time of King Josiah, he wanted to hold out the hope that even yet the 'lost' brothers might be restored, that unity might prevail once more over 'all Israel'.

4 Joshua's farewell speech   *Read Joshua 23:1–16*

Towards the end of his life, Joshua gathers the people and their leaders together for his farewell address. We are not told where this assembly took place, but the sanctuary at Shiloh (see 18:1) is perhaps intended. The book of Joshua began with the inaugural speech of the new leader. Now it ends with his final sermon (ch. 23) and exhortation (ch. 24). A comparison can be made once more with the life of Moses. The final chapters of Deuteronomy recount the last words of the lawgiver, his 'last will and testament'. This chapter functions in much the same way, and both the vocabulary and the themes are very similar. It seems probable that the same editor or editors who produced the final version of Deuteronomy were also responsible for the final editing of Joshua, as well as of the following history books.

The sermon emphasizes the continuing promises of God, but combines this with a clear warning of the need for covenant faithfulness. Verse 6 explicitly mentions the 'book of the law', echoing the words in 1:8, as well as the description of Moses depositing the book beside the ark of the covenant (Deuteronomy 31:26). On the one hand, the message is upbeat, with reference to the nations that God has already driven out (v. 4). On the other hand, there are strong words of warning of the dangers that lurk from the nations that still remain (v. 7). These warnings were needed, for the Israelites were, time and time again, captivated by the allure of Canaanite culture, customs and religious and sexual norms.

In many ways, this chapter provides a guide for reading the rest of the Deuteronomistic history work. The book of Judges recounts the backsliding of the tribes, the subsequent troubles they faced and the saviours or judges whom God raised up for them. 1 and 2 Samuel tell of the demand for a king so that Israel could be like the rest of the nations (1 Samuel 8:5). 1 and 2 Kings detail the loss of sovereignty, first by the eastern and northern tribes culminating in the deportation by the Assyrians in 722BC. This was followed by the fall of the southern kingdom and the capture of Jerusalem by the Babylonians in 587BC. The 'good land' (v. 16), the promised land, had become a lost land. The authors of Joshua and the other history books looked back to the early days of the Conquest as a time of wonder. Joshua's sermon, then, was meant not just for his own day but for all subsequent generations to hear and to heed.

5 'Choose this day' *Read Joshua 24:1–15*

The final action of the book takes place at the site of the altar at Shechem. Little has been said about Shechem so far, but it was an important sanctuary in the central hill-country. It was situated near to the two imposing hills of Ebal and Gerizim (see 8:30–35). The site had played a part in the stories of the patriarchs. Abraham built an altar there on first entering the promised land (Genesis 12:7) and Jacob also built an altar there (Genesis 33:18–20).

Some scholars think that the description of the ceremony at Shechem may reflect a tradition of covenant renewal in ancient Israel. Some argue, on the basis of Deuteronomy 31:10–13, that such assemblies took place every seven years. At these times the people would pledge themselves to serve the Lord. Whether that is true or not, this story in Joshua 24 provides a model for later generations to pledge their allegiance to God.

Covenants or treaties were common in the ancient world, binding two parties together. Often they were between a victorious king and his weaker neighbour or 'vassal'. Many of the features of these treaties are found also in the biblical covenants. One of these features is the 'history lesson', the review of what has led up to the signing of the treaty. In verses 2–13 the author relates, through Joshua's speech, the great deeds that God has performed. Beginning with Abraham and his offspring, the story goes on through the escape from Egypt, the desert wanderings and the conquest of the land of Canaan. Similar recitations of the 'marvellous works' of God can be found in some of the Psalms, such as 78, 105 and 136.

On the basis of this affirmation, Joshua offers a challenge to the assembly (vv. 14–15). God is faithful and to be trusted, but he demands total loyalty—no rival 'gods' may share his glory. So all other 'gods' must be put away, just as the first of the Ten Commandments demands (Exodus 20:3). The people must now make a choice between two false options and one true one. They could turn back to the ancient gods worshipped by their ancestors in Mesopotamia. Or they could start to worship the gods of the land of Canaan, whose powers are supposed to produce fertility for the land. Joshua ends with a challenge: 'Choose this day whom you will serve'. He himself has no doubt: 'As for me and my household, we will serve the Lord'. The gauntlet has been thrown down. How will the people respond?

6 The end of an era   Read Joshua 24:16–33

The response from the people is overwhelmingly positive. They affirm their willingness to serve the saving, liberating God who has led them from the slavery of Egypt to the freedom of the promised land. Surprisingly, perhaps, Joshua cautions them to think again. Do they really know what they are doing? He reminds them of two essential qualities of the God of the covenant. He is both 'holy' and 'jealous' (v. 19). Joshua warns them not to make promises they do not intend to keep.

It may well be that today we also are liable to make sacred commitments too glibly, without thinking through the implications. It is far too easy sometimes to 'go through the motions' in our worship services, and to mouth the words of our liturgies. The Methodist tradition, to which I belong, has the custom of a renewal of commitment in an annual Covenant Service. The covenant promise is demanding, even terrifying. Perhaps those people who choose to stay away on that Sunday are being more honest than those who say the words but do not act on them!

Covenant treaties in the ancient world were concluded in two ways—firstly by calling witnesses to attest the ceremony, and secondly by depositing the treaty at the local shrine. Both of these things take place. The people act as witnesses against themselves (v. 22) and the covenant details are written in the 'book of the law' and a memorial stone is set up at Shechem (v. 26).

The book ends with the description of three burials—firstly, that of Joshua, who is buried in his own inheritance within the tribal territory of Ephraim. Then mention is made of the burial of Joseph's bones, which had been carried all the way from Egypt. They are finally laid to rest in the plot of land Jacob bought at Shechem (v. 32). Lastly, verse 33 records the death of Eleazar, the priest. With these deaths the 'era of the conquest' comes to a close. Soon it will be followed by the turbulent and chequered period of the Judges. But that is another story, and the book of Joshua ends on a positive note. The stress is on the faithfulness of Joshua's generation to the great promises made at Shechem (v. 31). For the final editors of the book, it marked the end of a golden age.

GUIDELINES

The final chapters of the book of Joshua have shown how a new society was developed in the land of promise. The old Canaanite system of city states was swept away by the new and more equal system of the Hebrew tribes. Systems of justice and mercy were established through the cities of refuge (ch. 20) and through the levitical cities (ch. 21). Problems within the new community that could have led to division were dealt with carefully (ch. 22). Finally, when the land was at rest (23:1), Joshua could assemble the people, address them (ch. 23) and initiate the covenant in the promised land (ch. 24).

Yet the rest given under Joshua was only temporary, as the author of Hebrews 4:8 points out. Well over a thousand years after the conquest, another who bore the name Joshua/Jeshua would be born. For the author of Hebrews, it was the new Joshua, Jesus of Nazareth, who would provide the true rest for God's people. This new Joshua would have battles to fight against giants even more fierce than the Anakim—the ogres of sin and death. He would be, like his namesake of old, a champion and a conqueror who would call his people into a new covenant faithfulness (Mark 14:24). Ultimately, Jesus would lead his people across the waters of death and into the inheritance of eternal life.

Eternal God, thank you for the story of promises fulfilled in the land of promise. May we, like Joshua of old, be loyal in your service and ready to commit ourselves to live as your covenant people. We ask it in the name of the new Joshua, Jesus Christ our Lord. Amen

Further reading

A.H.W. Curtis, *Joshua*, OT Guides, Sheffield Academic Press, 1994.

E.J. Hamlin, *Joshua: Inheriting the Land*, International Theological Commentary, Handsel Press, 1983.

J. Gray, *Joshua, Judges, Ruth*, New Century Bible, Marshall Morgan and Scott, 1986.

J.A. Soggin, *Joshua*, Old Testament Library, SCM Press, 1972.

M.H. Woudstra, *The Book of Joshua*, New International Commentary on the OT, Eerdmans, 1981.

Living Jubilee

People interested in who is reading the Bible, and why, may have noticed one curious development in the last decade. An obscure chapter in the book of Leviticus has been dusted off and sent into action in the service of debt relief for the poorest countries of the world. At the time of writing (Autumn 1999), church activists under the banner of the 'Jubilee 2000' campaign have achieved a promise from world leaders of tens of billions of pounds of debt relief. It may not be fast enough or, simply, *enough* to save the lives at stake. Full debt relief, freedom for slaves and land reform may still be distant jubilee hopes. But we start the millennium with a glimpse of how these hopes may come to be realities.

Committed action and reflection on debt pulls us into wider issues of life and faith. In both cases, the process exposes some of the death-dealing powers that cause poverty and worsen inequality. The most committed campaigners now join a battle against entrenched interests of corruption and anti-democratic forces in both rich and poor countries.

Committed reflection similarly extends from thoughtful reading of Leviticus 25 to more entrenched issues of power. The codes for covenant worship and holiness in Leviticus and Deuteronomy affirm orderly worship of God, not just because this is God's due. Rather, right worship corrects the distortions of power and impoverishment in human societies. And so, debt stories are about issues of death-dealing power and oppression—realities that Christian faith meets with grace, freedom and redemption.

We read these ancient stories in a modern world in which faith is challenged by poverty; where a billion people get by (if they can) on about sixty pence a day. Over the next two weeks, we start with debt to reflect on issues of our faith and life. Or, if you prefer, we start in the red to reflect on redemption.

These notes are based on the New Revised Standard Version of the Bible.

1   From scarcity to abundance   *Read 2 Kings 4:1–7*

1 and 2 Kings, together with 1 and 2 Samuel, comprise a single work in four books in ancient Greek texts, entitled 'Concerning the Kingdoms'. Scholars group this work with Deuteronomy, Joshua and Judges and suggest that its editing shows a consistent point of view. Throughout the narrative, prophets try to keep rulers and people mindful of covenant faithfulness.

Here we get a glimpse, as if through a window of their house, into the lives of one family in the ancient world. Through the window, we see a single mother who bears the anxious weight of hunger and fear for her children, who are threatened with slavery because of debts she cannot pay (v. 1). She suffers what we sometimes call 'biblical poverty', by which we usually mean appalling destitution. Debts, and slavery related to debt, were one of the chief causes of biblical poverty. And so it is in houses like this where the study and practice of jubilee begin.

The story opens with a cry for help from wretched vulnerability. Her case is the worst nightmare for everyone who faces a future of economic uncertainty (and most of us, at some time, fear that we will). There are powerful contemporary echoes in this story. Statistics show that as health and education budgets are slashed to pay foreign debt, it is women who pick up the burdens, providing extra care in hospitals when there is no staff, even bringing in sheets and food for the patients. Women walk longer distances for antenatal care when clinics are closed, and care for sick children when drugs are scarce. The Anglican Mothers' Union reports from Nigeria the results of a poll of rural households to determine the effects of debt:

- *85 per cent of families in one poll had cut their meals from three to two a day.*

- *Almost a third had cut their number of meals to one.*

- *95 per cent of households had cut back on milk for the children.*

In today's reading, God worked through the prophet Elisha and confronted fear, scarcity, slavery and death head-on. Surprisingly,

Elisha starts with what the widow has, rather than with what he has brought. In the face of overwhelming odds, there is some encouragement that God can start with what we bring and transform it. The 'little' could be material resources, or emotional ones like energy and hope. The result: a miracle of abundance, freedom and life.

2 A downward spiral *Read Genesis 47:13–21*

The Genesis story begins to widen out from Abraham to the story of Israel's ancestors and their context—here, a downward spiral into landlessness and slavery. How does power get concentrated and inequality deepen in the first place? Here, those who are vulnerable to begin with find that one catastrophic setback—crops failing—hits them so hard that they lose their land and get deeper and deeper into debt. This is the cycle of impoverishment and finally enslavement that the later Jubilee laws are intended to reverse, with freedom for slaves, remission of debts, and the return of the land. Commentators are not sure whether Joseph's brothers were exempted from this process of enslavement, or whether this is a parallel explanation for the enslavement of the Israelites to the one offered in Exodus 1:8.

When the people run out of money during a famine (v. 14), they sell livestock, their only liquid assets (vv. 16–17). But livestock in a rural economy is also insurance for the future. Having mortgaged their future, they are reduced to selling their land (forfeiting the means of livelihood of the next generation) and, finally, can only barter with their bodies and their labour (v. 18). In fact, the downward spiral here is all too applicable to the hundreds of millions of present-day families who live without household insurance or access to health care that is free at the point of delivery. Poor families in Brazil tell how the long-term illness of one member can pitch the whole family into debt and ultimately lead to the loss of their land. Floods in Bangladesh cause a much higher death toll than floods of equal force in Florida; in the latter, homes are sturdier and resources at every level support the displaced.

In fact, living close to the edge of survival is almost a definition of poverty. Jesuit theologian Jon Sobrino watched the process in El Salvador and observed, 'The poor are those who are close to death—unjust and unnecessary death.' The Jubilee laws were intended to make life less precarious and more secure for those who were close to death.

3 The cry of the people *Read Exodus 5:1–19*

Here at the beginning of the Exodus story—before the escape from Egypt, or the establishment of the covenant—is a second succinct and incisive study of power. The Israelites are forced to produce without having the means, and punished for failing—details of an arbitrary and brutal reign of unchecked power against the weak. And there are familiar charges laid against the poorest and most vulnerable (in this text the hardest working people)—that they are lazy (vv. 8, 17). God has heard the people; they are to be free *from* this hostile, malicious distortion of power. What are they to be free *for*? To worship God (v. 3). Even in the act of liberation, God is defining the relationship he intends to have with the people who will be free. Liberating acts have their right context in a proper relationship with God.

Pharaoh's approach (v. 9, 'work harder') may be recognizable today, most disastrously for the poor in the policies imposed by officials the World Bank and International Monetary Fund over the last two decades. The gist of these policies is that poor countries must earn more and spend less.

For people who know what it is like to pay off their countries' debts, it feels like being told to make bricks without straw. The debt relief coalition Jubilee 2000 reports that Tanzania was $US 8 billion in debt in 1998, up from $5 billion in 1988. The country pays one third of its export earnings every year to service its debt, and its people suffer cuts to health and education, rises in basic food prices and the lack of credit and investment available in their communities. And the debt is still not paid. If every Tanzanian paid $200 (by going without food or clothes, for that is the whole of the average per capita income) at the end of the year, he or she would still owe $66. Rogate Mshana of the Evangelical Church of Tanzania reckons that this is slavery, 'not in the most primitive way of putting people in chains. Now you are putting them in economic chains without them understanding what you are doing to them'.

At first sight, this is an odd text to inspire the momentum that has written off billions of pounds of poor-country debt. Compared to Deuteronomy 15, it doesn't even focus very much on debt specifically (v. 37). This passage is set in the Wilderness period in the context of the 'Holiness Code' (starting at Leviticus 16) from which about half of the laws of the Torah were taken. The book is principally concerned with right worship of God, and how the Israelites might remain pure.

In fact, Deuteronomy 15 mentions debt more, but Leviticus 25 is the more significant because of the appearance of the concept of the Jubilee year, deepening and extending the observance of the Sabbath. It concerns the restoration of the land to its original owners, fair dealings in trade and not making profits from destitute family members. In contrast with the precarious survival of the poor, these laws are given to enable God's people to dwell on the land securely (vv. 15, 19).

As far as we know, this legislation was never enforced. In fact, during the reign of Herod the Great (40–4BC), Rabbi Hillel instigated a legal formula that enabled creditors to collect debts even after the Jubilee year. This was partly to keep credit lines open to the poor, as creditors might be reluctant to lend if redemption day was near. The result was much the same as it is with easily available credit now—more loans but endless, mounting debt for the poor.

Given its limitations then, what is it possible to extract from this text for a modern reader? There are at least two insights here. First, the principle that ownership of land ultimately rests with God (v. 23). The reason that the land should not be sold endlessly is that this would mean an inevitable concentration of ownership, contrary to its true provenance and authority, God. Second, its context in Leviticus introduces a profound truth of Hebrew scripture, that the health of our faith is bound up with that of the wider communities in which we play a role. Put simply, relationship with God is (at least in part) demonstrated in relationships with neighbours.

Luis Alberto Garcia, a community worker in El Salvador, reflects on the need for jubilee today with the contemporary truth of the

Leviticus passage: 'It is in this moment that the year of the Lord's grace should be announced. We must remind the powerful of this world that they can't become owners or take power over human life, nor of the planet itself. All we have, all that is here, is God's. It belongs to God and no one else.'

5 Open hands   *Read Deuteronomy 15:1–15*

These commands are given in the wilderness, following on from the Leviticus material and continuing the theme of what it means to be a people who worship one God in a covenant relationship. The people's relationship to God and God's own character are revealed by the saving act from slavery in Egypt: God is the one who saves, and they are the ones who were saved (v. 15). This act of redemption means that they will act towards God and others differently, so that history does not repeat itself by allowing the cycle of impoverishment and debt slavery to continue.

The American New Testament scholar Ched Myers writes in *Sojourners* magazine:

> *The Bible recognizes that inequalities will inevitably arise in fallen society—a realism it shares with modern capitalism. But the biblical vision refuses to stipulate that injustice is therefore a permanent condition. Instead, God's people are instructed to dismantle, on a regular basis, the fundamental patterns and structures of stratified wealth and power, so that there is enough for everyone.*

The jubilee laws here remind God's people that they were created for a purpose and freed for a purpose.

There are difficulties, however. What should modern Christians make of verses 3 and 6, which seem to exclude non-Hebrews from the benefits extended to community members? The final verse in this passage seems to extend the provision to others in the land (see v. 11). Christians will read this passage in light of the teaching of Jesus in (for example) Luke 10. After satisfactorily quoting Deuteronomic law, a lawyer then asks, 'But who is my neighbour?' Jesus tells the story of a good Samaritan—shocking in the context of the more exclusive law in which the lawyer has been schooled.

6   The poor press for change   *Read Nehemiah 5:1–12*

Here is a story, not of a miracle but of harnessing political will to enact something like jubilee debt-forgiveness. Some scholars allow that this is one time when the Jubilee may have been enacted. Notice the sequence of events. First the people speak at length (vv. 1–5). Then Nehemiah takes up their cause, moved to anger by their suffering and their eloquence.

Here on the lips of the poor must be one of the most searching texts in the scriptures. They protest at their oppression at the hands of the wealthy because, as they say, 'our flesh is the same as their flesh; our children are the same as their children' (v. 5). Here they assumed that they were all Hebrew people and therefore social equals before God. As we have discussed above, Christian tradition later extends this standard of social equality to include all people in light of a gospel message intended for all nations.

The radical nature of this text lies in its challenge to the community to consider inequality, rather than poverty. Clive Robinson, Senior Policy Adviser at Christian Aid, is an expert in what is called 'food security' for the hundreds of millions of people who face chronic seasonal hunger. As the term implies, food security is about stable, secure access to food, rather than one-off emergency parcels. It involves changes in government policies within countries and better terms of trade for the poor, for example in the prices paid for coffee or tea. In fact, stable access to food for the poorest almost invariably involves changes of priorities for the wealthy and powerful. Out of this experience, he argues that we should stop thinking in terms of 'poverty'. Instead we should think in terms of 'inequality'. Why? Because, as he observes, 'It is possible to say, *they* are poor. But we have to say, *we* are unequal.'

GUIDELINES

If '*we* are unequal', jubilee practices are measures by which we can judge our relationships in communities at every level—between slavery and bonded labour, creditors and debtors, 'haves' and 'have nots'. The distortions associated with inequality expose how far societies have fallen short of God's intentions. The Hebrew scriptures tell us that order has been perverted because we have forgotten who and whose we are. A searching exploration of debt leaves us with this question: who (or what) is *our* redeemer?

1 I know that my redeemer lives   Read Luke 1:67–79

This is an ecstatic vision of redemption, firmly in the tradition of the Hebrew scriptures. The evangelist underlines continuity with David (v. 69), holy prophets (v. 70), other ancestors who received the covenant promises in the laws of Moses (Deuteronomic law, v. 72), and finally Abraham (v. 73). Notice that here, as in the Pentateuch, the redemption has a purpose: 'that we... might serve him without fear, in holiness and righteousness' (v. 73). In fact, it is the same motif as the ancient exodus story established. Redemption is to reestablish worship of the true God.

Zechariah's song contains an announcement within an announcement. Zechariah focuses on John's role as a prophet in the line of covenant people he has just named (vv. 76–77). But the overall subject of the prophecy is something else—that a redeemer is near. In ancient times, a redeemer was a patron who paid off the debt that would keep the debtors from bondage and prison, or their children from slavery. As Peter Selby notes in *Grace and Mortgage* (DLT, 1997), it is easy to forget the economic reality behind the key metaphors of Christian faith. Exploring material and financial aspects of redemption can engage us in practical faith responses. These have implications for us, and for those who are both politically weak and poor.

2 Audacious words   Read Luke 4:16–22

Jesus announces that the time of freedom has arrived. He is the agent both of God's judgment and liberation from oppression, in terms that echo Zechariah's prophecy. In the context of this study, though, there are at least two difficulties with this text.

First, was Jesus referring to the Jubilee to announce redemption? Scholars are divided. He was certainly using the language of release and freedom, echoing familiar teachings for Jewish hearers of his message ('release to the captives' harks back to Leviticus 25:10). And there is an intriguing historical context for this language. The contemporary Jewish historian Josephus reports that about thirty years after the death of Jesus, 'A young hothead called Simon Bar Gloria took advantage of the breakdown in the political order, set up camp in the Judean hill country, and proclaimed liberty for the slaves and rewards for the free, so collecting the scum of the whole district' (*Jewish War* 2:425). Proclaiming liberty to the slaves is hardly innocent language in the New Testament: it certainly implies political and material change for the poor.

Jesus' promise hints at the second difficulty with the text, especially for readers for whom oppression seems endless and resistant to change. South African Christians in a poor black community in Durban in 1986 asked hard questions of this text: 'How was this meant?' And even harder: 'Is it true?' Some scholars say that Jesus extended the Hebrew scriptures from a reference to one historical event to a change of priorities and attitudes. The Revd Peter West of Christian Aid writes:

> *Perhaps Jesus deliberately refuses to give a blueprint... a jubilee liberation is not confined to one year, but persists against all attempts to suppress it, until all the earth is free, not confined to one nation only, but drawing all peoples into its dynamic energy.*

The South African Bible study decided that the key was in verse 21: 'Today the scripture has been fulfilled *in your hearing*' (emphasis added). The South Africans decided that as they heard and did what Jesus implied, the scripture was fulfilled.

3   **A response to grace**   *Read Luke 19:1–10*

Some scholars say that Zacchaeus was the chief tax collector in Jericho, and that many tax-collecting posts were open to the highest bidder. A licence to collect taxes would have been lucrative: ordinary people had to pay a variety of civil and religious taxes—personal, estate, customs duties, and religious taxes such as an annual tithe, a second tithe every third year and a temple tax.

It is difficult to condemn Zacchaeus from the standpoint of our own culture, in which the values of acquisitive ambition are so highly prized. In a society in which wealth was stratified and the middle class virtually non-existent, tax collecting might have offered a rare opportunity for some social mobility. But Zacchaeus represents and propagates the growing inequality and impoverishment of ordinary people in Jesus' day. Even the most scrupulous tax collector would have been tainted in Jewish eyes as a collaborator with Rome. But even worse, Zacchaeus has apparently broken Hebrew law by committing fraud. Tax collectors were paid by commission on levies raised and so had every incentive to boost the total by dishonest means.

Here, the 'sinner' (v. 7) goes straight to the heart of the gospel by an immediate shift of allegiances, and an immediate restoration of his (financial) relationships with the community. Zacchaeus identifies the chief barrier to his faith, and resolutely acts on it. It is a jubilee response, in the spirit of Leviticus and Deuteronomy, to liberation by a gracious God. The Bishop of Bradwell, Laurie Green, wrote in *Jesus and Jubilee*:

> *The Jubilee release of which Jesus spoke (in Luke 4) was not to be enacted every fifty years, but was now to be understood as a continuing state of mind, a metanoia, a repentance... so when Zacchaeus is welcomed into the Kingdom by Jesus, he immediately recognizes that since he has now experienced Jubilee release, he must in turn release those he has made indebted to him.*

Luis Alberto Garcia of El Salvador, from the perspective of a poor community in El Salvador, also looks for a deeper shift of allegiances as one of the ends of the Jubilee 2000 debt campaign. More than a one-off campaign, he says, it 'has to be a search for the conversion of all humanity, a sign of hope for everyone in which the rich will also benefit' (Interview, 1997).

4 Impossible possibilities *Read Luke 18:18–26*

By contrast with the tax collector, this 'ruler' has all the trappings of propriety and good standing in the community—the proper approach to Jesus the rabbi, combined with knowledge and awareness of the Law. But Jesus identifies his possessions as the obstacle to a life that has eternal significance.

From one point of view, Jesus' demand seems a bit harsh. Zacchaeus, after all, kept *half* of his goods. Jesus does not demand the same of all his followers in the Gospels. But those of us who are relatively wealthy cannot glance away from this text with the confidence that it has no relevance for us. Wealth is an obstacle to faith, as Jesus remarks in verses 23–27.

John Hull, professor of Religious Education at Birmingham University, in a probing study to identify barriers to faith, has identified the grip of money as the chief barrier to the development of adult Christian learning. And it is possible that, for some of us, it might be rather more serious than a barrier to faith.

In fact, we know, as profoundly as the people who wrote the Bible, what it is like to be in the grip of money as a god. Peter Selby writes in *Proclaim Liberty: Reflections on Theology and Debt* (Christian Aid, 1998) that his personal journey to try to understand the debt crisis led him to a troubling awareness of the power of money to claim the authority that should belong only to God.

> *Increasingly I see the citizens of the world's more affluent countries come to believe in money as the only adequate security in life and the only proper measure of the value of persons and ideas… Everywhere there are signs that the power and quantity of money is changing our behaviour, and that our beliefs are conforming to the behaviour that seems to be expected. The language of accounting, or investment and profit, encroaches on ever greater areas of our lives. More and more, the signs are that money comes to be seen as the saviour from a dangerous future, and the judge between our courses of action in the present.*
>
> *Saviour and Judge. Are not these the attributes of Jesus Christ, and only of him? Is not what we see a process that can only be called the divinization of money?*

For those of us whose behaviour and attachments may be at odds with our professions of faith, Jesus has a searching challenge. He has no illusions about how difficult it is for many of us to separate ourselves from our possessions for the sake of our faith (vv. 24–25). But with God's help, he says, it is possible (v. 27).

5 The Lord's Prayer and our money   *Read Matthew 6:9–13*

Surely Jesus was not talking about literal, financial debts in the Lord's Prayer? Increasingly, it seems that we must admit that possibility. First, because of the language. The Greek word for 'sins' in this prayer is consistent in Matthew (see 18:23–35, the parable of the unforgiving slave—tomorrow's reading). Intriguingly, Luke uses the words for debts and sins as if they were interchangeable: 'Forgive us our sins, for we ourselves forgive everyone indebted to us' (Luke 11:4).

The second reason we might question our assumptions about this text is that modern scholarship shows that many of Jesus' listeners would have been anxious about debt. We often say that the power of Jesus' teaching was his ability to relate faith to ordinary life. Debt (and perhaps taxes, as above) was a fact of life for most ordinary listeners. In fact, debt was literally a burning issue. Only thirty years after the death of Jesus, Jewish revolutionaries set fire to the house of the high priest Ananias and then 'took their fire to the record office, eager to destroy the money lender's bonds, and to make impossible the recovery of debts, in order to secure an army of debtors' (Josephus). 'Forgive us our debts' means 'money debts' because that would have been the straightforward and clear sense for the hearers of the prayer in Jesus' day.

Finally, it makes sense if we look at the structure of the prayer. Prayer for bread and freedom from debt are subsections of the broad petition, 'Your kingdom come'. In other words, the presence of bread and the absence of debt would be two signs of God's kingdom. Tom Wright puts it this way:

> *Among the many meanings that this had for Jesus' followers was that they were to practise the great old biblical command of Jubilee. Not only were they to forgive one another their sins and offences, they would have no debts from each other... You may say that since the debt we owe to God is moral and not financial, Jesus must have been using a metaphor. That is sometimes the case, but we can't escape the question so easily.*

The Lord and His Prayer, *SPCK, 1996, pp. 55–56*

6 Unforgiven? *Read Matthew 18:23–35*

A familiar story raises new issues in light of the global debt crisis. Why doesn't the servant forgive the one who owes him so much less? A very common reaction to the proposals of Jubilee 2000 is that debts should be paid off regardless and that it is wrong to write off debts. Is this always the case? What is the biblical witness on debt write-offs?

This parable can stimulate reflection on what may block forgiveness. Revd Ceri Lewis, of Trinity United Reformed Church in Wimbledon, has suggested: 'Maybe the unjust steward does not forgive because he himself does not feel forgiven. He is still, in his mind, trying to pay off a vast and unpayable debt' (unpublished sermon). According to this reading, Lewis says, the parable points to a God whose nature is to forgive, not according to the size of the debt but according to need.

If and when we do feel it, the gracious work of God can prompt an exhilarated response. George Herbert wrote:

> *Thou that hast given so much to me,*
> *Give one thing more, a grateful heart…*
> *Not thankful when it pleaseth me:*
> *As if thy blessings had spare days:*
> *But such a heart, whose pulse may be*
> *Thy praise.*

Our response to grace may be a private matter. But churches, as African American social critic Cornell West observes, 'may be the last places left in our culture that can engage the public conversation with non-market values' (unpublished lecture). Reflection on grace and debt in our own lives can inform our starting points as we confront issues of public policy. And these are life-and-death issues for the poorest people in the world that God loves so much.

GUIDELINES

What might it mean to 'practise the great old Biblical command of Jubilee?' (Tom Wright). Among other things, the Jubilee texts still challenge us to resolve our own faith priorities. A study of debt can lead us into a Bible where people testify to the power of money and the possibility that we can be free from it. And the Bible leads us into the world where we know all too well this power, and we need to hear that we can be free.

With God's help, we can pray:

From my poverty and my wealth
I will give, act and pray for Jubilee
and witness to God's good news
for the poor: release from unpayable debts
for the rich: freedom from the power of money.

Further reading

Susan Hawley (ed.) *Proclaim Liberty: Reflections on Theology and Debt*, Christian Aid, 1998.

Rebecca Dudley, *Living Jubilee: ideas for reflection and action*, Christian Aid, 2000 (available free).

Jesus in Paul's letters

Paul is the earliest contributor to the New Testament. He had been the fiercest opponent of the new Jewish sect—a zealous persecutor who had tried to destroy the Church (Galatians 1:13; Philippians 3:6). But he had received a divine revelation while in full flight as a persecutor. He was convinced that Jesus had appeared to him, risen from the dead (1 Corinthians 15:8). He felt himself called to preach this Jesus among the Gentiles (Galatians 1:15–16). His conversion resulted in the transformation of the earliest Christian mission, and the spread of the new faith through the northern Mediterranean world and into Europe. Were it not for Paul, there might never have been Christianity as we know it, and Europe might never have become a Christian continent.

What Paul believed about Jesus, then, is of first importance for Christians. Paul's belief not only transformed Paul himself but also shaped the language of Christian faith for all time. Over the next two weeks, therefore, we shall look at some of the key passages that Paul wrote (or quoted) about Jesus, and thus attempt to build up a rounded summary of his belief.

The first week, we will concentrate where Paul seems to have concentrated—on the significance of Jesus' death and resurrection as the core of Christianity's distinctive beliefs, which caused it to become a distinctive sect and then a separate religion. The second week will broaden out to include the fuller ramifications of this core belief.

Throughout, the richness and diversity of the imagery should be noted and entered into as far as possible. The diversity of the imagery, even when strange to us, tells us that the first Christians had a deep experience of Christ and appreciation of what he had done which they were determined to express as fully as they could.

1   Paul introduces himself   *Read Romans 1:3–4*

Paul was writing here to a church which he had not founded and which he had never before visited. As letters like Galatians and 1 Corinthians indicate, Paul's reputation was rather controversial in some quarters of the early Church. So he takes the opportunity given by the opening section of the letter to introduce himself to his readers in Rome.

It is significant, then, that he inserts into his more typical greeting this brief snatch of 'the gospel'. This was his 'calling card'. It was the gospel that would provide the link and bond between them. Evidently he wanted to reassure the Roman congregations with regard to his understanding of the gospel. It was not his nationality or his social status that would count with them. And although he mentions his apostleship (1:1), he does not make a great deal of it, since he did not regard himself as the apostolic founder of the Roman churches (cf. 1 Corinthians 9:1–2). What counted was the gospel: if the gospel that he brought was one and the same as the gospel which had called them into existence as churches, he would be welcome.

So Paul quotes what, it would appear, was already a summary statement of the gospel, one which was probably widely known (cf. 2 Timothy 2:8). This is one of the functions of shared statements of faith—that they make a bond between those who share them. That's probably why it is best that such statements are kept brief and are not elaborated too much. The more detail they go into, the more disagreement they provoke, and the less they are able to serve as a basis for union.

The two lines of the confessional statement highlight two central points for Christian faith regarding Jesus. One is what is later described as his 'humanity'. The second is about his 'divinity'. Important to note about the first is Jesus' Jewishness. Jesus was a Jew, whom Christians believe to be the Messiah expected by Israel. That remains a central element in Christian belief about Jesus. The other emphasizes the importance of the resurrection. The resurrection saw Jesus 'appointed as Son of God in power'. That is where distinctive Christian belief about Jesus begins. These two beliefs remain at the core of all Christian faith.

2   The earliest statement of faith   *Read 1 Corinthians 15:1–8*

When casual conversation turns to Christianity, a question that often arises is, 'When did distinctive Christian beliefs about Jesus first emerge?' The claims made about Jesus are crucial to Christianity, and mind-blowing in themselves. They are the sort of claims that one might have expected to develop over a lengthy period, their origins lost in the mists of myth and legend. There were many tales about gods and goddesses circulating in the Mediterranean world two millennia ago, few if any of which would be regarded as credible today. So, is Christianity any different?

This is where this passage assumes a major importance. The first letter to the Corinthians was written probably in the early 50s of the first century. And here Paul cites the faith in which he himself had been instructed when he first became a Christian. We know that Paul's conversion must have taken place sometime within three or even two years of Jesus' crucifixion, that is, roughly twenty years earlier. It would be simply impossible to fit in all the events and timing of Paul's career on a later dating. In other words, in this passage we are taken back to (probably) within two years of the events described. Here is the central Christian testimony already well established and recorded within a matter of months of the events that gave rise to these beliefs.

Again there are two principal features in the statement. The first is that 'Christ died for our sins in accordance with the scriptures'. This belief in the significance of Jesus' death ('for our sins') was not an afterthought, or a product of long reflection and intensive debate among the first believers. His death was seen as fundamental to the process of 'being saved'.

The second is, once again, Jesus' resurrection. But here, what is of particular interest is the parade of witnesses that Paul marshals. The resurrection of Jesus was not simply wishful thinking, a deduction drawn from some scripture. Jesus was seen again, 'appeared', showed himself to many individuals. And not just to Cephas (Peter) and the Twelve, but to more than five hundred at one time—'most of whom are still alive' and able to confirm the testimony. This was not something done in a corner.

3 A perpetual embarrassment *Read 1 Corinthians 1:21–25*

The last thing the people of Israel wanted was to be told of a Messiah who had been crucified. 'Messiah' means 'anointed one', one set apart and commissioned by God for a special purpose. The popular hope had been that God would send such a specially anointed one to restore David's kingdom, to liberate the land of Israel from Roman rule, and to preside over a reunited and prosperous people. But a Messiah who was put to death? And death by crucifixion? No!

Crucifixion was a shocking death. No Roman citizen would be crucified. It was a form of execution reserved for slaves and traitors. How could a Jew be expected to believe in a Messiah who had been crucified? The very suggestion was like a great boulder on the pathway, over which one could not avoid stumbling. And in the mind of Gentiles, who regarded themselves as more sophisticated, the very thought was a nonsense, a mere foolishness.

But Paul did not flinch in the face of such response. This embarrassment, this stumbling-block, this foolishness, was actually the key to a new way of looking at reality, a new system of values. The world which saw crucifixion as nothing but an unmitigated disaster was also the world which valued noble birth as something intrinsically good, which valued money as the test of worth, which valued clever speech as the mark of wisdom. But the cross does not devalue Jesus. Rather, Jesus revalues the cross. And with the cross he revalues that whole set of human assumptions that saw the cross as only an embarrassment.

That is why Christianity adopted the cross as its symbol—not the nice gilt crosses that make badges and brooches and glittering ornaments on church buildings, but the cross of rough timber, nails and blood, the cross of execution, the cross of humiliation, the cross of embarrassment. The temptation will always be present to Christianity to pretend that the embarrassment is not there, to replace the crudity and ugliness of the cross with its gilt counterfeit, to conform to the world with its different values. But the crucified Christ is still the foolishness of God—and, as such, still wiser than human wisdom.

4   The cursed Christ   *Read Galatians 3:13–14*

The thought of crucifixion was horrific enough. But it signified something still worse for most Jews. Deuteronomy 21:23 says that the body of the criminal hung on a tree (following execution) was regarded as accursed by God: 'anyone hung on a tree is under God's curse'. But in the decades before Jesus' death, this text had come to be applied to those who were crucified—crucifixion understood as being 'hanged on a tree' (as in Acts 5:30). So one of the objections no doubt brought against earliest Christian preaching of the cross was that Jesus' death proved him to have been cursed by God.

This text from Galatians shows how the first Christians reacted to this charge. They did not deny it! They accepted it! Jesus had been cursed by God! How could they do this?

The logic is given in verse 14: '…in order that in Christ Jesus the blessing of Abraham might come to the Gentiles'. Somehow the barrier that had prevented the blessing of Abraham coming to the Gentiles had been removed by the cross. How so?

The answer must lie in the Torah, the Law of Moses. Among other functions, the Law served to protect Israel from the negative influences of other nations, whose religious, social and moral standards were not reckoned as so high. It protected the holiness and purity of Israel as the chosen people. That was why, as in Deuteronomy 21:23, the criminal's corpse must be removed before sundown; otherwise it would 'defile the land'. So Jesus' death on the cross could be regarded as one of those defiling factors. In other words, the crucified Christ became like the other nations, the Gentiles, as a factor which threatened Israel's set-apartness to God.

The point, then, is that by raising Jesus from the dead, God had indicated his acceptance of this Jesus, this crucified Christ—his acceptance of this Christ judged by the law to be accursed. He had turned upside down the logic that defined Gentile as impure and crucified as accursed, the logic that required Jew and Gentile to remain separate, the logic that had limited the blessing of

Abraham to Israel alone. God accepts the accursed; he blesses the Gentile.

5 Just like sinful flesh *Read Romans 8:1–4*

Romans 8:3 contains one of the most tightly packed descriptions of the incarnation and its purpose. Here we highlight only two aspects of it.

First, the incarnation itself. There was a problem about humankind, or Israel in particular. They had been given the Law. That is, they knew what God wanted; they knew what to do—but they couldn't do it. As flesh, they were weak. The flesh—is physically weak; it is subject to decay through age, to disease and accident. 'Flesh' in Paul also indicates moral and spiritual weakness. Here the weakness is human dependence on its appetites being satisfied. In Paul's terms (but not his alone), human desire craves for satisfaction, and that craving can often become unhealthily strong; it can turn to lust (Paul provides an earlier summary of the point in Romans 7:5). It is this weakness of the flesh that opens the door to sin (Romans 7:7–13), weakens the law and prevents its fulfilment (7:14–25).

God's way of dealing with this impasse was to send Jesus in the very likeness of that flesh, weak as it was, and prey as it was to the temptations of sin. Here, in other words, Paul rules out any suggestion that Jesus the man was essentially different from the rest of humankind. On the contrary, he was just like us. He knew the weakness of the human condition, the strength of human desire and the subtle attractions of sin, just like all the rest of us.

Second, the purpose of his mission was 'for sin'—'to deal with sin'. The same phrase is used in the Old Testament to describe the sin offering. The function of the sin offering was to put away sin, that the sinner might be forgiven, his or her sin 'covered' (Leviticus 4—5). Jesus' death, then, is depicted as a sin offering on behalf of all human flesh. Somehow it dealt with the crippling weakness of human flesh, and the power of sin which made the law so impotent. Somehow Jesus' death (and resurrection) released a new power (the Holy Spirit), which transformed that older weakness into a new way of life (v. 4), and transformed the law of sin and death into the law of the Spirit of life (v. 2).

2 Corinthians 5:21 provides another angle on earliest Christian understanding of Jesus' death. No doubt this is what Paul is referring to when he speaks of God making 'him to be sin who knew no sin'. For this could hardly be other than a description of Jesus' death as sin offering, or, in particular, as the sin offering and scapegoat of the annual Day of Atonement (Leviticus 16). In that ceremony, the high priest laid his hands on two goats. One was sacrificed in the usual way. But on this occasion its blood was taken into the innermost sanctuary, the Holy of Holies, and there sprinkled on the lid of the ark of the covenant (the mercy seat). The other was driven off into the wilderness and there left to die.

Explicitly of the second goat it is said that the high priest's laying on of hands signified the putting of all Israel's sins on the head of the goat (Leviticus 16:21). In other words, the goat was 'made to be sin'. And since the sacrificial animal had to be pure and without blemish, it could be said that the high priest 'made it to be sin that knew no sin'. Probably this is what the laying on of hands signified in all sin offerings—although the point is disputed. It is certainly significant that both in the Dead Sea Scrolls and in later rabbinic writings, the same significance is attributed to each goat. Almost certainly, then, the tradition drawn on by Paul in 2 Corinthians 5 understands Jesus' death as a sin offering and/or scapegoat.

More to the point, the tradition helps us to understand how the sin offering was thought to 'work'. It 'worked' by transferring the sin confessed on to the sin offering. The sin offering, now embodying the sin, dealt with the sin by its death; by its death the sin offering destroyed the sin. The one who offered the sin offering, with the sin removed and eliminated, was thereby restored to full relationship with God.

Paul puts the point in terms of 'reconciliation' (sin constituting a breach with God) and 'righteousness' (the reconciled relationship is the right relationship which God seeks with his people). Individuals avail themselves of this reconciliation by identifying themselves with this sin offering—as it were, putting their hands on Jesus and confessing their sins over him.

Our readings this week have concentrated on the heart of Paul's belief in the crucified and risen Christ. But for Paul, it was never enough simply to believe that 'Jesus died for our sins' and that 'God raised him from the dead'. The earliest Christian confession—'Jesus is Lord' (Romans 10:9), a confession made publicly in baptism—was not merely a matter of words. 'Lord' also indicated 'Master': to confess 'Jesus is Lord' was therefore to put oneself under this new Master, to confess Jesus as *my* Lord, to accept the status of Jesus' slave. The point is that a slave, by definition, did not belong to him or herself. A slave could not decide how to use his or her own time, but was always at the master's beck and call. To confess Jesus as Lord in baptism was therefore to hand oneself over to Jesus, for Jesus henceforth to direct and order one's life.

The public character of baptism would make the confession something from which there was no going back. It would mean not just a change of mind or habit, but perhaps the whole way of life. The change required might well be so radical that family would disown and friends reject. It could mean, quite literally, becoming a new person. In short, 'Jesus is Lord' was not some easy phrase to slip out without much thought; it indicated a lifelong (or life-shortening) commitment.

16–22 OCTOBER   THE GLORY OF GOD THE FATHER

1   At the name of Jesus   *Read Philippians 2:6–11*

One of the almost infallible marks of a living Christianity is its hymnody. Renewal in Christianity has always been accompanied by and expressed in singing new songs. It looks as though that has been the way from the first. Many scholars, for example, think that Philippians 2:6–11 was an early hymn. With the new faith in Jesus, it would be no wonder that hymns were composed in honour and praise of Jesus.

This one seems to praise Jesus under the image of a second

Adam (although the point is disputed). The first Adam, made in God's image (Genesis 1:27), had clutched at the chance to be like God, equal to God (Genesis 3:5). In consequence, it was a merely human likeness he passed on, a life subject to death (Romans 5:12). Christ had not repeated that first mistake, but none the less had freely followed Adam's path through human life to death. Because of this, God had exalted him and given him the dominion over the rest of creation that God had intended for humankind, the crown of his creation (Psalm 8:6). Hebrews 2:6–9 builds a similar meditation on the same passage from the psalm. Here, in other words, Jesus' life and death are caught up as the crucial parts of a much larger, universal story.

What is particularly interesting here is the language used of Jesus' exaltation following his death. In 2:10–11 the hymn echoes a passage from Isaiah 45:23. And what is so striking about that is that Isaiah 45:23 is part of one of the boldest and most emphatic statements about God as the only God in the whole of the Old Testament. The God who says, 'I am God, and there is no other' goes on to say also, 'To me every knee shall bow, every tongue shall swear' (45:22–23). But the Philippian hymn looks to the day when every knee shall bow and every tongue confess 'that Jesus Christ is Lord'. In other words, in Philippians Jesus is being given the honour which, in Isaiah, God claims for himself.

What an astonishing development for a strictly monotheist people to hail Jesus in terms reserved for God alone! But notice: Paul adds, 'to the glory of God the Father'. Jesus, the second Adam, more than fulfils God's purpose for humankind, but still does not usurp God's glory.

2   Jesus the intercessor   *Read Romans 8:31–34*

One of the great images for Christ is that of priest. Many readers will be familiar with the classic threefold imagery of Christ as prophet, priest and king. In fact, however, the image of Jesus as priest is made little use of in the New Testament—with one exception. The exception is a large one: the epistle to the Hebrews makes Christ as priest the centre and focus of its whole presentation. But, interestingly enough, the image used is of a unique kind of priest—the priesthood of Melchizedek—a priesthood with no other members than the mysterious Melchizedek of Genesis 14:18–20 and Christ himself. And no wonder, when we see the qualifications for membership (Hebrews 7:3)!

The reason why the image did not naturally suggest itself is simple: Jesus was not of the tribe of Levi, not of the house of Aaron. He did not qualify as a priest. In contrast, he was of the tribe of Judah, and of the house of David. So Jesus as king was an obvious line to follow. And 'prophet' was not a regularized or institutionalized vocation. More or less anyone could be called prophet; it was a matter of inspiration, not of birth.

But there was more to it than that. For in the accounts of Jesus' betrayal and death, the opposition to Jesus is almost exclusively priestly in character. Likewise, in the first few chapters in Acts, it is the chief priests who lead the opposition. Very soon, also, we find something of a breach between the first Christians and the temple (Acts 6:14; 7:48). And elsewhere Paul spiritualizes temple imagery (e.g. 1 Corinthians 6:19) and speaks of everyday obligations as priestly sacrifice (Romans 12:1). So perhaps Paul was less keen on using priestly imagery for Christ.

Nevertheless, there is one passage where he cannot resist using it. In painting the wonderful scene of the last judgment, he draws on the picture of Jesus as God's principal adviser, who sits at God's right hand and 'intercedes for us' (as in Hebrews 7:25; 9:24). The imagery is a mixture of our 'counsel for the defence' and court chamberlain (grand vizier) through whom one is brought into the royal presence. We should not let the strangeness to us of the imagery dull its force and effectiveness.

3 Coming with clouds   *Read 1 Thessalonians 4:13–18*

Everyone is concerned about the end point. 'How will it all end?' is one of the questions most asked by those seriously worried about matters of government policy or about major decisions made by family or friends. And when one steps back and attempts to gain an overview of the whole sweep of history, the whole sweep of life, 'How will it end?' is an unavoidable question.

The first Christians asked it too. They asked it, not least, because they thought they had been given the answer. In Christ they had already seen the end. They had seen the Kingdom of

God, what God's rule would be like, what the end of God's purpose in creation and salvation would be. And so it was natural that they should express their hopes and expectations for the end of all things in terms of Christ, and particularly in terms of Christ's return.

Jesus had encouraged this sort of expectation. In several parables he had used the storyline of an important person going off for some time, and leaving work and responsibility behind, before returning to claim his due. The first Christians simply took up this storyline and applied it to Jesus himself. Jesus had gone off following his resurrection, but would assuredly soon return (Acts 3:19–21 is one of the earliest expressions of this conviction). In 1 Thessalonians Paul himself picks it up, perhaps using a prophetic utterance (4:15). Whatever its origin, Paul's imagery is a combination of the Son of Man figure in Daniel 7:13–14 and of the oriental city's welcome to a visiting king (the citizens going out to greet him).

In this case, the purpose was to comfort those whose loved ones had died since Paul's visit. Paul writes to give reassurance that those who died would not be disadvantaged in relation to those still alive when Jesus returned. The imagery will once again be strange to us, though we can be fully sympathetic with the purpose to which it is put. But the fundamental point remains: Christ already embodies the end point; he shows the character of the climax towards which God's history is moving. Whatever the imagery used, we can rest on that.

4   As at the beginning   *Read 1 Corinthians 8:4–6*

As earliest Christian thought tried to make sense of the end, so it tried to make sense of the beginning. And as it did so by reference to Christ in the one, so it did also by reference to Christ in the other. As Christ reassured as to the character of the end, so Christ provided insight into the character of the beginning. The Christ who embodied God's purpose for the end also embodied God's purpose from the beginning.

One of the earliest expressions of this is 1 Corinthians 8:6. Paul's Jewish forebears had used the figure of divine wisdom to express the equivalent conviction (e.g. Proverbs 8:22–31): God

71

created the world wisely; the wisdom evident in the beauty and regularity of creation was the wisdom of God; that same wisdom could be most clearly accessed in the Torah (Law) (Ecclesiasticus 24:23). Taking up this line of thought, the first Christians simply applied it to Christ: the wisdom behind creation is now most clearly seen in and accessed through Christ; he is God's wisdom (1 Corinthians 1:24, 30).

Some of this may seem abstruse to us today. But the point being made in this way was of first importance. For it prevented a frightening split that became dominant in other religious systems and often threatened Christianity in subsequent centuries. This was the split between creation and salvation, between physical matter and spirit. Some religious systems can only see physicality or materiality as bad, as evil; to be saved is to be saved from materiality; salvation is of the soul *from* the body. The consequences are frightening. Such a view glorifies strict asceticism, abhors sexuality, disregards the environment, and so on.

But Judaism and Christianity insist that the cosmos was created by God and is basically good. And by insisting that God created through Christ (and will complete through Christ), Christianity insists that salvation will be the restoration and completion of creation. The consequences are equivalently positive towards the body, towards sexuality and towards the environment. It is still worth insisting that Christ is the wisdom of God.

5 Jesus the exemplar *Read Romans 15:1–3; Galatians 6:1–2*

A feature that causes a lot of surprise is Paul's failure to say much, if anything, about Jesus' own life and ministry. He focuses so much on Jesus' death and resurrection. And we have seen how far his attempts to express Jesus' significance stretch—from the beginning of creation to its climactic end. But what of that period of Jesus' existence which attracts so much attention in the Gospels—his three years of ministry prior to his death? The references to that are few and far between.

Many deduce from this unexpected silence that Paul was not interested in Jesus' life and teaching. And there is a point worthy of consideration here, that is, that Paul did not think of Jesus primarily as a great teacher. His letters do not consist of meditations on things Jesus said or did (John's Gospel could be so described). Paul did not see himself as developing Jesus' insights, dotting the 'i's and crossing the 't's, as it were. His was a gospel of redemption from the power of sin and the weakness of the flesh.

Nevertheless, Paul did not ignore Jesus' own teaching. There are quite a number of allusions to it (as here). The difference is that he did not see any need to teach it; rather he assumes it. We may assume that Paul did not intend his letters as a means of teaching the sort of 'Jesus tradition' we find in the Gospels. That must have been taught by other means, as when a new church was founded (using what we may call 'foundation traditions'), with teachers appointed to preserve and instruct (e.g. Galatians 6:6). When Paul said things like 1 Corinthians 13:2 ('If I have all faith… but do not have love') and 1 Thessalonians 5:2 ('The day of the Lord will come like a thief in the night'), he presumably expected the shock of recognition of something Jesus had said to reinforce his point.

In today's passages, Paul has echoed Jesus' teaching on love of neighbour (see also Romans 13:8–10 and Galatians 5:14, which allude to Mark 12:31). In both passages he sees concern for the fellow Christian as key examples of such neighbour love (explicitly Romans 15:2). And Jesus provides not only the teaching, but also the example—of one who did not please himself but the neighbour (Romans 15:3). By 'the law of Christ' (Galatians 6:2), Paul presumably has the same combination in mind—the law of love as taught by Christ and as lived out by Christ in his ministry with and for the poor and sinners.

6 Christ who lives in me *Read Galatians 2:19–21*

This passage represents one of the most astonishing turns that Paul's references to Jesus take. Christians are generally so familiar with it that they no longer see it as strange—which is a pity, since it is just its strangeness which would normally cause us to pause and reflect on it a good deal longer than we do.

I refer to the thought of Christ 'living in me'. In fact, much the more usual way of speaking in Paul is of the believer living 'in Christ'—a phrase which occurs many times in his letters. But the two phrases are evidently part of the same conceptuality, as a comparison between Romans 6:3–11 and 8:9–11 confirms. The conceptuality is well caught in the German word *Ineinander*, 'in-each-otherness'. Paul and the recipients of his letters evidently experienced an integratedness between Christ and themselves, a symbiotic relation between the two. Hence also the image of the church as 'the body of Christ'. The language was not simply some fancy theory to be believed on. Paul, at any rate, experienced it. He did not see himself as his own master. There was, indeed, another living in him, motivating him, enabling him. That power source, replacing and competing with the old power source of weak flesh and selfish desire, is what gave Paul his fantastic vision and drive.

The motif is more complex in Paul. For in effect he sets Christ's life, death and resurrection as a kind of template on which his own career is being drawn. His turning (conversion) from a way of religion and life dominated by the Law he saw as a re-enactment of the crucifixion in his own life (Galatians 2:19). There was no hope for the old Paul except through crucifixion with Christ. And the process would not be sudden or overnight: the tense implies a lifelong transformation (see also Romans 8:17; Philippians 3:10–11). The resurrection of the body would be the individual end point of the process (Romans 8:10–11, 23).

Quite how Paul held together the different images of Christ the intercessor, soon coming on the clouds, and 'Christ in me', 'the body of Christ', we cannot now say. But here we need to recognize Paul's consciousness of Christ as a transforming power working in and through him.

GUIDELINES

The focus on Jesus is so intense in the New Testament that it is easy for a Christianity which is based exclusively on the New Testament to slip into a kind of Christolatry. One of the most ancient heresies was that of Modalism, or Monarchianism. This claimed that the one God had been manifest first as the God of the Old Testament, then as Jesus and finally as the Spirit. Some Christian groups who seem to forget about God the Father are in danger of falling into this ancient trap. The most obvious alternative was to claim that Jesus was a second God. And, truth to tell, there are many Christians who think they are good

Trinitarians, but whose attempts to spell out their faith actually express a form of Tritheism—God as three 'persons', with 'person' understood as you and I are persons.

Paul seems to have been aware of such dangers. In 1 Corinthians 15:25, he writes of Christ's reigning 'until he has put all his enemies under his feet'. This is an allusion to one of the most fundamental texts on which Christian understanding of Jesus' resurrection was based—Psalm 110:1: 'The Lord says to my lord, Sit at my right hand until I make your enemies your footstool.' Jesus was the 'Lord' to whom the Lord God had said, 'Sit at my right hand until I make your enemies your footstool'. This implied that to hail Jesus as 'Lord' was not to be seen as any kind of challenge to God as Lord. Rather, Jesus was Lord as one who had been given to share in God's Lordship.

For all his devotion to Jesus Christ, Paul remains a monotheist. He remains a monist: there is only one divine principle behind and within and over the world. Christ is the fullest expression and embodiment of that principle. But he is not the principle itself. Only God is 'all in all' (1 Corinthians 15:28). Jesus in Paul's writings always brings us to God.

Habakkuk: from fear to faith

It is never easy to introduce someone about whom we know practically nothing. Habakkuk's name, unusually for a Hebrew, does not give any clue as to his character or background, and he does not mention his personal life. However, his prophecy gives us some clues about him. The 'Chaldeans' (1:6) are the Babylonians, and they are beginning to make their power felt. The Assyrian Empire, which conquered the ten northern tribes of Israel in 721BC, is declining or has already been overcome, and Babylon (modern Iraq) is the latest aggressor, threatening tiny Judah as well as larger countries. So we can probably place Habakkuk towards the end of the seventh century BC, most likely in the reign of the weak and vacillating king Jehoiakim, who paid tribute to Egypt and Babylon in turn, and ended his life with a foolish act of rebellion (2 Kings 23:34—24:7).

Habakkuk is concerned with dangers from outside and with injustice and oppression in his own country. The 'oracle' he sees (1:1) can also mean 'burden'; Jerome wrote that the word 'never occurs except when it is evidently grave and full of weight and labour'. Finally, Habakkuk is a poet: the last chapter (assuming it is his work and not a later addition) has much in common with the Psalms.

So we come to this desperately burdened prophet, gifted as a writer, living in uncertain times, clear-sighted enough to see the shortcomings of his own nation as well as those of others, and certain that he has a message which he must give, because it is God's message.

These notes are based on the New Revised Standard Version but can be read with other translations.

23–29 OCTOBER

---

1   **Question and answer**   *Read Habakkuk 1:1–11*

'How long,' Habakkuk asks God, 'must I keep on praying? And why do you not listen to me?'

God's silence is perplexing and frustrating. Wrongdoing, destruction and violence flourish in an atmosphere of 'strife and contention'. The law seems powerless ('slack' in verse 4 can mean 'paralysed'). The 'wicked' (godless) outnumber the 'righteous' (faithful), so the minority are persecuted by the majority and any attempt at justice becomes corrupted. Why must Habakkuk dwell upon such a situation? How indeed can God bear to look at it?

The response (vv. 5–11) does not give the solution for which Habakkuk hopes. Instead, God invites him to widen his vision: 'Look... and see'. The sight of 'the nations'—the Gentiles—is not reassuring: 'Be astonished! Be astounded!' can be translated, 'Shudder and be shocked.' The prospects are frightening. The Babylonians are on the move, and there is no reason to think that they will be less savage than the Assyrians. Arrogance and speed are their outstanding characteristics. They are aggressive and ruthless and they make up their own rules as they go along, based on their own power and pride. Their advance is compared to the swiftest and cruellest animals and birds (v. 8). They press on relentlessly and gather up captives in numbers like grains of sand. Existing rulers and kingdoms are only a laughing-stock to them (v. 10).

This does not seem a comforting answer—or any answer at all, until we look more carefully. First, it is God who is mobilizing the Chaldeans. It is not the first time that he has used a foreign nation—the Assyrians have already been the 'rod of his anger' (Isaiah 10:5). Second, the Babylonians themselves will not escape God's judgment. At present, 'their own might is their god' (v. 11), but nations rise and fall, and their gods fall with them.

Overall, God is in control of the forces of history; unlike other kingdoms, his kingdom is secure. This will not be easy for Habakkuk to believe in the coming storm, but it is the unchangeable truth.

2   Question without answer   *Read Habakkuk 1:12–17*

The full, dreadful truth dawns on Habakkuk. The Babylonians are to be the instrument of God's judgment, not on a sinful world in general, but on Judah itself. The prophet's complaint against his own people is being taken up in a way that he views with horror.

However, he affirms that, whatever happens, God is 'from everlasting' (in contrast to the Chaldeans who are of comparatively recent origin). Moreover, he is the prophet's God, 'holy' or set apart, distinct from all other gods, and indestructible. ('You shall not die' is sometimes rendered 'We shall not die'—either way it is a vote of confidence in the future.) And yet this faithful, unchanging one has marked out a heathen and ruthless nation to deal with his covenant people (v. 12).

How can this be? God cannot even contemplate evil, but he says and does nothing when the wicked overwhelm a people who, however corrupt, are not in the same class when it comes to sheer depravity (v. 13). It is hard to face the fact that God's purity passes judgment on all sin—whether it is somewhere 'out there', or whether it is at home.

Verses 14–17 describe the extent of the destruction which God allows and apparently condones. People who are his creation, even his chosen people, provide prey for the tyrants who, like monstrous fishermen, trawl the nations indiscriminately, exulting in their wrongdoing and even worshipping not only their own might but also their weapons of destruction.

Now comes the next question: not only 'Why?' but also, again, 'How long?' (v. 17). It is hard to believe, in the middle of all this trouble, that Babylon's power will come to an end. A horrifying immediate prospect does not encourage anyone to take the long view.

These questions about the nature of God are the ones we still ask, and there is no indication that they are unacceptable to him. Even Jesus, on the cross, cried, 'My God, my God, why have you forsaken me?' (Matthew 27:46). Perhaps hardest of all is having to wait, as Habakkuk waited, for an answer and still affirm, as he did, that God is our God, and that he will in his time bring about justice.

3   Watching, waiting and writing   *Read Habakkuk 2:1–5*

Having again challenged God, Habakkuk settles down to await his next answer. He sees himself as a watchman whose job is to patrol the city walls, keeping watch for any danger that will threaten the people. This is a lonely and a responsible task: Ezekiel (33:1–9), comparing prophets to watchmen, reminds them that if their words go unheeded they are not blameworthy, but that if they fail to give warning they will bear the responsibility for the coming catastrophe. However, Habakkuk is looking not for trouble but for any sign that God is answering his prayers.

When the word comes (v. 2) it is to be written down in clear, bold letters, 'so that a runner may read it'. This may mean that it must be intelligible to anyone rushing by, like one of today's billboards, or that whoever reads it may run with it, and presumably spread the news. It will be in the form of a vision of 'the end', either of Babylon or of the end of time, when God will finally judge his enemies. It is hard to watch and wait; it is always easier to talk or to act; but God's answers, though certain, only come in God's time.

The message is both serious and reassuring (vv. 3–4). Those who have no relationship with God are puffed up with their own importance, and crooked in their ways, because—needing to appear self-sufficient—they are less than truthful. There is no future for them; they are intoxicated with their own success; their greed is insatiable: like death itself, who never takes time off, they cannot be satisfied but are always looking for more. This picture of the marauding Babylonians can be applied to a wider canvas— to all restless, dissatisfied souls who look to earthly values to bring them happiness and satisfaction.

By contrast, those who are 'righteous', that is, right with God, do not need to struggle to justify themselves. 'The just shall live by faith' (v. 4), the great words that changed Martin Luther's life, point forward to the assurance that our salvation does not come by our own efforts but by the work of Christ (Ephesians 2:8–9), and remind us that in our daily lives there is still the need for faithfulness—the perseverance and commitment involved in walking 'by faith, not by sight'.

4 Tragedy and silence *Read Habakkuk 2:6–20*

Five 'taunts' or 'riddles' ('wise sayings') are directed at those who have rejected the words of 2:4, 'The righteous live by their faith'. The immediate targets are contemporary powers—Babylonian or Jewish—and idolaters, but the words apply to all times, nations and individuals, and the subjects of judgment will be not the oppressed but the oppressors.

'Alas' can be translated 'Woe'. The exact meaning lies somewhere between the two; there is an element both of God's judgment and of his grief, for he must condemn wickedness yet still loves its perpetrators. What is it that breaks God's heart? Throughout the catalogue of wrongdoing, we must remember that as well as crimes against humanity, devastation of the environment is condemned (vv. 8, 17). God's concern is with his whole creation. And retribution comes not by national or personal vengeance, but from God himself. 'Vengeance is mine, I will repay,' says the Lord (Romans 12:19).

The first 'woe' is extortion (vv. 6–8). Territorial expansion, exploitation of people and resources, and encouragement to get deep into debt are characteristic of greedy nations and individuals. But the situation will suddenly reverse; the 'debtors' will become 'creditors' and call in the debts which their persecutors owe.

Second (vv. 9–11), the house or dynasty that is built by means of ill-gotten gains will not flourish—the very fabric of the project, impregnated as it is with evil, will become the instrument of judgment.

Third (vv. 12–14), the city whose building has been founded on bloodshed and crime will likewise come to a sad end. The onlooker may see splendour, but God sees violence, and the whole enterprise will be consigned to the flames—a waste of time and effort. Yet there is hope. When the kingdom of God comes (v. 14), not only will wrongs be put right, but his visible presence, his 'glory', will permeate the earth, and all will 'know' him in the deepest, most intimate sense.

Fourth (vv. 14–17), those who degrade others will themselves be degraded. Verse 15 is probably only one example of how self-respect is deliberately destroyed; the consequence will be that guilty nations and individuals will in their turn be forced to drink —but from God's own cup of judgment.

Fifth (vv. 18–19), idols are simultaneously lifeless and powerful, because those who make them allow them to become the focal point of their lives and set their standards for living.

But above the shouts of the destroyers, the cries of the sufferers, the babble of the idolaters, comes the command, 'Keep silence!'

(v. 20). God still reigns supreme over the world, and our response must be silent awe. He is greater than any of the calamities that have been so vividly described.

5   A psalm of prayer and praise   *Read Habakkuk 3:1–15*

'Shigionoth' (v. 1) 'Selah' (vv. 3, 9, 13) and 'To the choirmaster' (v. 19) all suggest that this poem, like the psalms, became at some time part of Israel's regular worship, probably at the autumn Feast of Tabernacles, looking back to Israel's journey through the desert and forward to God's provision for the following year.

Habakkuk has come a long way since his first prayer. Now, instead of asking, 'How long?' he looks back at God's work in the past, and prays that in the present he will renew it, reveal it and, even in the midst of righteous anger, 'show mercy'—a word denoting love of great depth. The prophet who speaks God's word to his people is, for the moment, also the intercessor who pleads with God on behalf of his people.

Reflection follows petition: what has God done which is relevant to this moment? Verses 3–5 describe him on the move: he comes not from Jerusalem but from Teman and Mount Paran in the south—areas through which Israel passed on their way from Egypt to Mount Sinai after the exodus. His glory and majesty are almost indescribable (v. 4); and his judgment comes to all (v. 5). His power is absolute; the mountains and the Bedouin tents of Cushan and Midian (both past enemies of Israel) are alike shaken at his presence.

After this picture of deliverance and destruction comes one of victory over chaos. In the ancient world, creation was seen as a battle with the forces of confusion and disorder, but, unlike the gods of Canaan, God does not vent his anger on nature; he is in control of it, as he was when Israel crossed the Red Sea (v. 8). The violence of the imagery in verses 8–12 reflects the fierce storms which from time to time swept Israel; Habakkuk's hearers would recognize these pictures.

In verses 13 and 14, the ultimate purpose of God's mighty acts is stated clearly—the deliverance of his people and the destruction of their enemies. In some way the latter will be self-inflicted; they will destroy themselves with their own weapons. Throughout, the significance of creation and of the exodus have been intermingled. God is sovereign over both the earth and its history.

6 Challenged and changed   *Read Habakkuk 3:16–19*

Having sought God in prayer, Habakkuk has had a profound experience of God's majesty, and his reaction marks a turning point in their relationship. He is shattered by what he has seen. Every part of him, physical and emotional ('I tremble within' describes his deepest, innermost feelings), is overwhelmed. His response confirms that it will be 'a fearful thing to fall into the hands of the living God' (Hebrews 10:31).

Habakkuk's weakness and fear come from contemplating 'the day of calamity'—not only the disaster which threatens his own people, but the judgment which will come on the Babylonians. He who has been horrified by their cruelty and aggression is now awestruck by the certainly of their ultimate destruction.

But he does not remain in this state of near collapse. Once he cried, 'How long?' (1:2); now he 'waits quietly'—he can rest, knowing that however long the wait may be (and its duration is not revealed to him), God's purposes will be accomplished. To hand everything over to God brings release from all kinds of tensions.

However, this waiting is not passive. In verse 17 Habakkuk faces up to a scenario not easily understood by those living in the modern, industrialized West. He finds the courage to ask, 'But what if...?' He contemplates total disaster—no grain, oil, wine, wool, meat or indeed food of any kind, fruit, cereals or milk. And into this situation will come a brutal invading army. Yet, given this prospect, he makes a deliberate decision. He will still rejoice (or 'triumph') and exult (literally 'be excited')—not in material blessings, because they do not exist, but in God himself, who is the Saviour both of his people (v. 13) and of his servant. True joy does not depend on outward signs of God's blessing, but on the unseen, constant presence of God himself.

So Habakkuk can say confidently that God, not his own resource, is his strength, and that although the way ahead may be hard and long, he will, like the nimble deer, move surely through the dangerous terrain.

GUIDELINES

Habakkuk has made an exhausting journey from questioning and fear, through the traumatic realization of what is going to happen in the short term, to the longer perspective of the eternal nature of God's power and presence. His final state of heart and mind could be expressed by these words:

My goal is God himself, not joy, nor peace,
Nor even blessing, but himself, my God;
'Tis his to lead me there—not mine, but his—
At any cost, dear Lord, by any road.

F. Brook

A month for remembering

November is an important month in the life of the church. All Saints Day, All Souls Day and Remembrance Day fall in the first half of November, to remind us of a vital dimension of our faith. Part of what it means to be members of one another in the body of Christ is to be able to draw strength from those who have gone before us in the faith. There is more to this than the power of mere example. Because space and time do not limit the love of God, there is a sense in which the people of God in all times and places are bound together in one great fellowship—the communion of saints. The beginning of November helps us to remember this.

This month also draws our attention to the element of sacrifice—pouring out life for the sake of others—that is found throughout human experience, and especially in war. Remembrance Day is a most poignant reminder. Many of the saints in the church's calendar have followed the example of Jesus literally, by giving their lives for their faith. November asks us to consider the part played by sacrifice in our faith.

These readings can be used with any version of the Bible.

---

30 OCTOBER–5 NOVEMBER   **REMEMBERING,**
                                    BELIEVING, LIVING

---

1   **Heroes of the faith**   *Read Hebrews 12:1–3*

The Western church has celebrated All Saints Day on 1 November since the ninth century. Its origins lie in the earlier remembrance of otherwise uncommemorated martyrs by the churches in Syria and Rome during the Easter season. All Saints Day gives us the opportunity to recall some of the heroes of our faith: men and women who have inspired others in the way of Christ.

The short passage from Hebrews 12 comes at the climax of a recalling of some biblical heroes of faith—Abel, Enoch, Noah, Abraham, Moses, Rahab the prostitute, Gideon, Barak, Samson, Jephthah, David, Samuel, the prophets and a host of unnamed people, women and men, whose abiding qualities seem to have been endurance and hope. 'Of [them] the world was not worthy' (Hebrews 11:38).

For the writer of Hebrews, the saints are not simply figures from the past. We are invited to imagine them as a 'great cloud of witnesses', like spectators at an athletics event, cheering us on to 'run with perseverance the race that is set before us' (12:1). The Christian life is not a lonely pilgrimage to the heavenly city, because 'you have come... to the assembly of the firstborn who are enrolled in heaven' (that is, the people of faith who share in the inheritance of Jesus the firstborn) and to 'the spirits of the righteous made perfect' (that is, the souls or spirits of the faithful departed) (Hebrews 12:22–23). Whatever else this means, it expresses in a vivid and imaginative way what we say regularly in the Apostles' Creed: 'I believe in the communion of saints.'

All Saints Day reminds us that the Christian experience is indeed one of communion—not only with God but also with those who, across time and space, have trusted him with their very lives. Living in an individualistic and fragmented culture can make it hard enough for us to appreciate the contribution made to our lives by those who lived only a generation ago. All Saints Day invites us to lift up our hearts and minds to celebrate all those who have gone before us in the faith of Jesus Christ. In a very real sense, their faith and devotion can still make a difference to the world—not least, through us.

2 How God blesses the world *Read Matthew 5:1–12*

'Birds of a feather stick together.' 'Like cleaves to like.' Popular sayings like these are full of conventional wisdom. Research shows how similar married couples are to one another, even down to their looks. Uniforms—whether official, like those of the school variety, or informal, like the obligatory brands of trainers and sweatshirts—promote cohesion by making people look the same. Unlike their nineteenth-century equivalents, modern towns are planned by offering people of similar economic status the chance to live side by side. Some of the most tragic news stories in recent years have shown how violence is used to rid whole areas of those who are 'not like us'.

Our similarities hold us together—the similarities of blood (family, tribe, race, nation), peer group, culture, history, and so on. Left to our own devices, we are 'birds of a feather'.

Today's passage from the opening of the Sermon on the Mount is often read on All Saints Day. Jesus tells us that God blesses the world by going against the grain of conventional wisdom. The poor in spirit, the humble, the mourners, the merciful, have only one thing in common: they know what it means to hang on to God in faith, and in so doing to support and sustain one another. God blesses the world by creating what Brother Roger of Taizé calls 'a people of the Beatitudes'—a communion of saints.

In increasingly mixed societies, in a disturbingly divided world, we can't hope to base our common life on what makes us the same as each other. That way, we become more tribal, more separated, more dangerous. The unifying qualities that Jesus looks for cross social, racial and even religious divides, and open up the possibility of a unity enriched by diversity. How then does God bless the world? Not by promoting similarity or separatism, but by creating a 'people of the Beatitudes'—a holy communion.

This suggests that what Christians experience as 'the communion of saints'—a community from all times and places that goes against the grain of conventional wisdom—is not an end in itself, but a pointer to the purpose of God for all people. That makes our celebration of All Saints Day vital for the renewal of the world.

3   Love without limit   *Read Romans 8:31–39*

As far as we know, the Christian Church has always commemorated those who have died in faith. Christian funeral services commend the faithful departed to God in the hope of sharing in the benefits of Christ's victory over death. From earliest times, the Church has remembered the departed at the eucharist on or near the anniversary of death. And there have been special days set apart for a general remembrance of those who have died: in the Syrian church, Holy Saturday was one such day. The observance of All Souls Day on 2 November goes back one thousand years.

What are we doing when we remember the faithful departed before God? Some Christians object to the idea of praying for the souls of the departed, as if they need our help to achieve salvation. Ideas like this can only undermine belief in the efficacy of the saving work of Christ. But it is possible to move beyond medieval ideas of intercession for the souls of the departed, and see All Souls Day as a chance to celebrate the power of the love of God to defy all that would limit it, including death.

This is to enter into the faith of Paul the apostle. Nothing in all creation has the power to separate us from the love of God that we have seen in Jesus Christ (vv. 38–39). Remember how Paul envisages that love: 'God proves his love for us in that while we were yet sinners, Christ died for us' (Romans 5:8). As far as God is concerned, people are worth loving, sacrificially. 'God's love has been poured into our hearts through the Holy Spirit that has been given to us' (Romans 5:5). God's love enters into the very depths of our being and conveys to us something of the character of the divine Lover—holiness, in the form of crucified love. All Souls Day reminds us that love like this allows nothing to limit its power to embrace those who live and die in Christ. 'Whether we live or die, we belong to the Lord' (Romans 14:8).

A prayer I sometimes use following a death or at a funeral captures the spirit of All Souls Day perfectly. This is how it starts:

> *We remember, Lord, the slenderness of the thread*
> *   that separates life from death*
> *and the suddenness with which it can be broken.*
> *Help us also to remember that on both sides of the divide*
> *we are surrounded by your love.*

4 The waste of war   *Read Ezekiel 37:1–14*

Since 1946, those who died in the great wars of the last century have been remembered on and around 11 November, the anniversary of the end of the First World War in 1918. Remembrance Day services are both church and civic/national events. The churches join with the wider community to mark the loss of so many lives. In recent years, the focus has broadened to include all who suffer as a result of war: civilian casualties, the relatives of those who died fighting, victims of the many violent conflicts in the world today.

Ezekiel 37:1–14—the valley of the dry bones—is in some ways an unlikely choice of passage for Remembrance Sunday, but it is there among the readings in one of the Church of England lectionaries. It would be easy to concentrate on the message of hope at the end: the Spirit of God breathes life into the dry bones, to symbolize the power of God to restore his people to life (vv. 12–14). But I want to draw attention to the early part of Ezekiel's vision. He sees a valley full of very dry bones (vv. 1–2), an image of the waste and tragedy of Israel's recent history. In the early part of the sixth century BC, those who lived in Jerusalem and the surrounding region were deported, and forced to live as refugees in a foreign land, Babylon. 'Our bones are dried up, and our hope is lost; we are cut off completely,' they complained (v. 11).

The story of Israel's exile is being replayed throughout the world, wherever violence and war create refugees and impose ethnic cleansing. It is foolish and wrong to assume that there are simple solutions to these issues. But that should not blind us to the sheer waste of life and resources involved. I am reminded of Geoffrey Studdert-Kennedy's poem, 'Waste'. Here he reflects on the devastation of a war that, among other things, wasted 'youth's most precious years', reducing 'muscle… brain… manhood… beauty' to nothing more than dried-up bones.

Television pictures bring many valleys of dry bones into our living rooms. Is it too much to hope that by reminding ourselves of the sheer wastefulness of war—as we do on Remembrance Sunday—we might limit the extent of war in our world?

5   No greater love   *Read John 15:9–17*

It is too easy to be sentimental about the sacrifice of life in war. Many—if not most—of those who die in war have no choice about laying down their lives. There is nothing particularly heroic about being in the wrong place when the bombs explode. Yet somehow the tragedy and waste of war still manage to create heroes, most of them unsung.

On Remembrance Sunday we are reminded of Jesus—victim of the tragedy of violence, the awful inhumanity of it all, the worst that human beings can do to one another, the waste. Yet unlike many others who suffer as a result of violence, Jesus had some choice in the matter. 'No one takes (my life) from me, but I lay it down of my own accord. I have power to lay it down, and I have power to take it up again. I have received this command from my Father' (John 10:18). The sacrifice of life is truly heroic when it is freely chosen.

Jesus died as the embodiment of the love he commended to others. 'Love one another as I have loved you. No one has greater love than this, to lay down one's life for one's friends' (John 15:12–13). The fruit of such loving is a community in which self-giving love is the touchstone of all that is good and true—something the Christian Church has not always found easy to remember. Love like this has the power to forgive enemies (those who inflict violence, of whatever kind), and even to overcome—or at least to absorb—violence. Christ-like love is the basis of a mysterious kind of peace: 'Peace I leave with you; my peace I give to you. I do not give to you as the world gives' (John 14:27).

The difficulty lies in imagining how this way of loving can make a difference in a world in which divisions are deep-rooted and violence has been nurtured over long generations. Only, perhaps, through a particularly heroic form of holiness.

6 Life poured out *Read John 12:20–28*

Towards the end of November, the cathedral to which I belong—St Edmundsbury Cathedral in Suffolk—celebrates its patronal festival. We recall the heroism of Edmund, king of the East Angles, who was martyred in 870 defending East Anglia from the invading armies of the Danes. According to his earliest biography, the Danes tied him to a tree and shot at him, so that he ended up looking like a porcupine. This is why he is often pictured holding an arrow. In about 900, his body was brought to Bedericesworth (later renamed Bury St Edmunds), where an earlier king of the East Angles had set up a monastery two hundred years before. By the time of the Norman conquest, the shrine of St Edmund had become a place of pilgrimage at the heart of a thriving town.

Martyrdom is, of course, a particularly heroic form of holiness, and one that is not confined to the past, when the defence of Christian faith mattered more than it appears to today. The church's calendar encourages us to remember those men and women who, down the centuries, have given their lives for the sake of Jesus Christ. Would we do the same? We hope we won't have to. But faith that is courageous enough to pour out its life for God demands our attention. Is it an example of the waste that Studdert-Kennedy saw in war? Or is it the fruitfulness of the seed that falls into the ground and dies?

The memory of Jesus the martyr lies at the heart of our faith. There is nothing in the Gospels to suggest that he had a masochistic streak in his personality, or that he expected this of his followers. Jesus seems to have enjoyed life to the full, so the sayings about loving and hating life (v. 25; cf. Mark 8:34–37) are about priorities rather than self-denial for its own sake. The martyrdom of Jesus was the fruit of his devotion to his Father: 'Father, glorify your name' (v. 28). This meant putting the cause of God's Kingdom before anything else; living out his own teaching; hungering and thirsting for the sake of righteousness, come what may (Matthew 5:6). Jesus' vision of the will and purpose of God clashed with the vested interests of those who lived by an alternative vision. We hardly need reminding of the outcome of Jesus' particularly heroic form of holiness.

All this is meant to inspire and encourage us. The fate of Jesus does not befall all his followers, though we are all drawn into his fruitful way of pouring out life for the sake of God and the world he loves. November is as good a month as any to remember what it is we are called to be and to become, as disciples of Jesus in today's world. Holiness—sainthood, the calling of *all* Christian people (Romans 1:7)—always has at least a grain of the heroic about it.

GUIDELINES

This week's readings have been about human remembering. But they leave out something fundamental. Our remembering is an image of God. God remembers, re-members—holds in his heart— the lives of all people at all times in all places. God's memory is an aspect of his love. And it makes it possible for us to remember creatively, joyfully, hopefully.

Almighty and eternal God,
you have kindled the flame of love in the hearts of the saints:
Grant to us the same faith and power of love,
that, as we rejoice in their triumphs,
we may be sustained by their example and fellowship;
Through Jesus Christ your Son our Lord,
who is alive and reigns with you,
in the unity of the Holy Spirit,
one God, now and for ever.

Collect for the Fourth Sunday before Advent

*If you enjoy your Guidelines
Bible reading notes, why not consider
giving a gift subscription to a friend
or a member of your family?*

*You will find a gift subscription order form
on page 157.*

The Gospel of Matthew
Chapters 9——18

In our previous readings in this Gospel, we found that Matthew
had given us important information concerning the true nature of
Jesus. Jesus' ethical teachings were introduced in the Sermon on
the Mount and we had come to the point where Jesus had begun
his ministry among the people.

This next section of the Gospel begins with Matthew
establishing the divine authority of Jesus by showing his mastery
of sickness, demons and the natural elements. The disciples begin
to ask questions about who Jesus really is.

6–12 NOVEMBER   **MATTHEW 9:1—10:42**

---

1   A paralytic man   *Read Matthew 9:1–8*

Jesus has returned from his excursion to the outskirts of Gentile
territory, to Capernaum, which Matthew infers is Jesus' home town.
His first encounter is with a group of people who carry between
them a paralysed man. The man is presented as too helpless to
move for himself, and dependent on the help of his friends. We find
the same story also in Mark (2:3–5) and Luke (5:18–20), but
Matthew omits some of the more colourful and commonly known
details of the story, such as the friends digging down through the
roof and lowering the paralysed man down to rest before Jesus.

Matthew instead prefers to concentrate on what he sees as the
main issue. Jesus notes the faith of the friends, how they believe
that Jesus can heal their friend. Then he says something quite curious, especially from our modern perspective. He tells the paralytic
man that his sins have been forgiven. The outcome of this is that
the man is healed, and is able to go home carrying the bed that
previously he was forced to lay upon.

The scribes do not see things the way Jesus does. In their eyes,
Jesus is a blasphemer, a man who has arrogantly assumed the
powers of God for himself. They are quick to condemn him for this

perceived offence, as they do not understand who stands before them.

This is the first time that Matthew has introduced the notion of forgiving sins in a healing story, and for him this is the heart of the story. The actual healing of the man is to show the reality of Jesus' authority to forgive sin. Matthew's deletion of the details of the story is designed to highlight this very point, to make it stand out and not become lost in the telling of the story.

Jesus' authority to forgive sin demonstrates clearly that the reign of God is at hand. In ancient Palestine, the presence of deformity or illness or mental disease was thought to be the physical manifestation of evil or sin. Jesus' ability to heal these problems shows how the power of God was penetrating into darkness and evil. Such healing is a sign of the imminent overpowering of sin, and proclaims the beginning of the kingdom of God.

2   Mercy and sacrifice   *Read Matthew 9:9–17*

This next section opens with Jesus walking along the road. He sees a tax collector, the man for whom this Gospel is named, sitting in his tax-booth. Jesus says, 'Follow me', and Matthew rises and does just that.

This word 'follow' is of great importance in the Gospel of Matthew. We first met the word in chapter 4, when Jesus commanded the disciples to leave their fishing profession and follow him. Like the fishermen before him, Matthew leaves his old life without hesitation to follow Jesus. His obedience to Jesus' call means a radical change of lifestyle for Matthew, where money and greed are replaced with dedication to the work of the Kingdom. Such a change of lifestyle in one considered a sinner would be seen by us today as a reason to rejoice. But here again we find some of Jesus' fellow Jews critical of his actions. To follow Jesus meant a life turned upside down, a life in which taking risks and associating with people of doubtful standing became the norm. It meant accepting the people that Jesus accepted—people considered to be 'bad company', including tax collectors, prostitutes and those reckoned to be unclean.

It may seem logical to us to find converts among those who sin rather than those who are already righteous. But Jesus comes under fire for his strange conduct, not only from the Jewish leadership but also from the disciples of John. The Pharisees had asked why Jesus ate with sinners; John's disciples want to know why Jesus eats at all. Should not a holy man fast? Jesus responds with the analogy of a wedding, where the guests feast and rejoice while the bridegroom is present. The presence of Jesus signals a new era, the time of fulfilment and rejoicing as God's Kingdom comes near. When Jesus is taken from them through crucifixion, then it will be the time for mourning and fasting. Thus, under these present circumstances, it is as foolish to continue traditional practices such as fasting as it would be to patch old clothes with new, unshrunk cloth, or to put new wine into old wineskins that can only burst under the circumstances.

Jesus recognized that bringing people to the Kingdom of God meant associating with those considered to be 'bad' company. It meant moving out of the conventional lifestyle and away from the places and people that one felt comfortable with, and taking risks. It meant a whole new way of being, a new life that was fitting for entry into the Kingdom of God.

3 Healing and faith   *Read Matthew 9:18–26*

This story begins the last group of healing miracles that we find in the Gospel. The collection of miracle stories continues the theme established in our last reading—the present time is one of blessing and rejoicing, for the bridegroom, Jesus, is present and demonstrating the great blessings that God's Kingdom will bring to those on earth.

Jesus is interrupted as he dines by the appearance of a respected community leader, who enters the house and kneels before him. He begs Jesus to come and lay his hand on his dead daughter, so that she can live again. Jesus gets up and, accompanied by his disciples, begins to follow the ruler to his house.

Before Jesus reaches the girl, his journey is interrupted. A woman seeking to be healed touches his cloak. Here again we see Jesus in contact with the unclean of society. Women were routinely segregated from men during religious devotion, and a woman who suffered continual bleeding was considered to be unclean, and defiling to any man she touched. Yet Jesus stops and says comforting words to her. As well as commending her faith, he addresses her as 'daughter'. Far from seeing her as unclean, he treats her with the care the ruler has shown for his own daughter. Her encounter with Jesus not only heals her but reinstates her in society.

Jesus continues his journey of healing. He arrives at the ruler's house to find many mourners lamenting the death of the little girl. Jesus commands the crowd to leave. They respond by laughing. As the bleeding woman modelled faith, so the members of this crowd show disbelief, and are cast outside for their pains. Jesus takes the little girl by the hand, and she gets up from her bed.

These two miracle stories go hand in hand. They again demonstrate the authority of Jesus. They also illustrate the profound changes that faith can bring out, a faith that trusts in Jesus' authority. The woman's simple but deep faith heals her. The father's faith in Jesus raises his daughter to life again. These healings symbolize a central belief of the Christian Church—that faith in the power of Jesus transforms people and leads them to new life. The girl finds life anew through her father's faith; the outcast and bleeding woman can now experience new life as a full member of society.

4 Many miracles   *Read Matthew 9:27–38*

In Matthew 9:9–17, we noted that the verb 'to follow' had special significance in Matthew's Gospel. In this next miracle story, Matthew tells us that the two blind men follow Jesus, so we are alerted that this healing story may be of special significance.

The two blind men cry out to Jesus, addressing him with the title 'Son of David'. Their cries remind us of the promises made concerning the true nature of Jesus: he is the promised 'Son of David' (1:1), the Messiah or Christ (1:16–17), and the true 'king of Israel' (2:2). Jesus questions them about their faith. Do they believe that he can do this thing? Their reply is simple but sure: 'Yes, Lord'. So Jesus touches their eyes and they see.

It is interesting to speculate why the blind men are so certain that Jesus is the one to help them. Perhaps they had heard that he was proclaiming the nearness of God's Kingdom and performing miracles of healing. Perhaps Jesus was their last chance to participate fully in the world around them. Whatever their reason, their faith in Jesus as the Christ is what counts. Their healing again reminds us of Jesus' power to transform.

This healing story is another example of how following Jesus involves a radical change in one's life. The blind men are not only healed of their affliction, but they become keen evangelists for the Kingdom, despite the fact that Jesus' commands them to tell no one else. Their faith and persistence changed their lives in real physical and spiritual ways. The blind men were once among those who walked in darkness (4:16); now they have literally received the light.

One of the last healing stories that Matthew records is the healing of the mute demoniac. Concerning the actual healing, Matthew merely reports that the demon was cast out. His focus is on the response of the crowds and the Pharisees. The crowd is amazed, and they state that the miracles of Jesus are a first for Israel. The Pharisees again fail to recognize what is really before them, and attempt to explain the miracles by accusing Jesus of consorting with the devil. It is not till later in the Gospel that Jesus will confront his accusers.

Jesus continues his ministry of healing and proclaiming the good news of God's Kingdom. The enormity of this task will lead him to send out his disciples on the same mission.

5 The mission begins *Read Matthew 10:1–15*

Jesus has just described himself as 'Lord of the harvest' (9:38). Now he summons his disciples and prepares to send them out on mission, as the labourers to help with the harvest. The disciples are given something of the authority Jesus himself has over evil spirits and sickness, so that they may continue to proclaim the Kingdom and demonstrate its nearness by restoring people to wholeness. Jesus also warns the disciples of the opposition and persecution that awaits them all at the hand of rulers and non-believers, the people who fail to recognize the authority from God.

Jesus begins his instructions with the charge that the disciples are to 'go nowhere among the Gentiles, and enter no town of the Samaritans', as their mission is directed towards 'the lost sheep of the house of Israel' (vv. 5–6). These are strange words to us, for traditionally the Church has believed and taught that God is God of all people. So why is Jesus so exclusive here? The position of the prohibition at the beginning of the disciples' mission suggests that it was of importance to Matthew, and not just a phase in the ministry of the historical Jesus that he was obliged to repeat. So how are we to understand it?

The disciples' task is to preach the coming of the Kingdom and to demonstrate its nearness by healing and exorcism. Time is of the essence, as the end-time judgment is fast approaching (10:23). The context strongly suggests that only Israel is envisaged as the mission field, because Israel was the people for whom the Messiah of the Jewish scriptures had been promised. Time was running out for Israel to accept Jesus as Messiah before the Day of Judgment arrived. For the people of the covenant, rejecting the Messiah of God was far worse than being a Gentile (10:15).

In this Gospel, Jesus, as leader of the lost sheep of Israel (9:36; 10:6; 15:24), is the one sent to turn the 'lost sheep' from following unrighteous and lawless leaders who will lead them astray. For Israel, entry to the Kingdom of God is by following the authoritative and truthful teaching of Jesus, as the fulfilment of the Law of Moses. As we have seen in the example of the centurion in chapter 8, righteous Gentiles are also welcome in the Kingdom, but the criteria for them seem to be different. On the Day of Judgment, they will be judged by their acts of kindness (25:31–42) and their belief in the authority of Jesus (8:5–13; 15:28).

6   Sheep and wolves   *Read Matthew 10:16–42*

Jesus now turns his attention to the trials and tribulations that the disciples will experience at the hands of Jewish councils and Gentile rulers. The picture that he paints is terrible and fearful. Hated by many, driven from town to town, the disciples will meet harsh oppression and punishment wherever they go. Yet there is still hope in the midst of all this projected fear and suffering. The disciples are told that they need not fear those who persecute them, and Jesus gives a number of reasons why this is the case.

First, although the disciples will be led before Jewish councils, Roman governors and kings to stand trial, this very persecution will present them with the opportunity to proclaim to them the gospel of the Kingdom. And even in this task, they are not to worry because the Holy Spirit will provide them with the right words.

Second, the disciples can take comfort in this rejection, for it means that they are like their teacher, Jesus. The picture painted here of the sufferings of the disciples reflects the events of Jesus' arrest and trial later in the Gospel. Jesus makes it clear that though the body can be killed, the soul cannot; if, like Jesus, they persist in adhering to their faith, their reward will be resurrection to the Kingdom of God.

To illustrate the care that God has for the life and soul of the disciples, Jesus reminds them that God has oversight and care even for creatures as small as sparrows. Jesus has once before in chapter 6 reminded them of God's care for even the most minute and unimportant of creatures, and how they are worth so much more to him. In fact, God knows them so well that God can even number the very hairs of their head. The trials in human courts ultimately mean nothing; it is the trial in God's court that will count for all eternity. Jesus is both advocate and prosecutor in this court, for he will acknowledge those who upheld his name, and deny those who did not.

Even today, God will surely look after the welfare of those who serve him. Though Christians may experience persecution or jeering or apathy or even death as they seek to proclaim the gospel, God will undoubtedly be with them, giving them courage and hope for the better future to come.

GUIDELINES

The miracle stories of Jesus still have the power to amaze us and remind us of the greatness and goodness of God's grace and power. To concentrate on the miracles themselves as central to Jesus' ministry, however, is to miss the point. The true nature of Jesus' ministry—the forgiveness of sin and the defeat of evil—is what undergirds the healing miracles. Jesus' healings are signs that sin and evil will be ultimately overpowered. However, for this to happen, and for the Kingdom to come with all its hope and wholeness, Jesus must first sacrifice himself through death on the cross.

When we examine the miracle stories in the context of the whole of the Gospel of Matthew, it is clear that for this author and his community, there can be no forgiveness of sin or healing without the cross. It is the cross, and not the miracles, which is central to the fundamental purpose of Jesus' ministry. It is from the cross that Jesus ultimately receives his authority to heal, forgive sin and proclaim the dawning of the Kingdom.

The miracle narratives are designed to be pointers that direct us toward the realities that lie at the heart of the Church's confession and tradition. The raising of the dead to life is a fundamental belief of the Christian Church, and reflects the confidence that God will raise believers from death at the end of time. The restoration to wholeness is the promise that is given by God to those who experience the transforming power of faith in Jesus. This wholeness need not be physical, but could be a sense of well-being and contentment within the spirit.

Thus, within these narratives, which we enjoy rereading and retelling in our churches today, lies something of our own individual experience as Christian and also the history of the Church. They reflect our hopes and our trust, and the power of the risen Jesus in our lives. They do not simply record past history, but also bring us face to face with our present experience. It is through such experience that we can trust in the promise of salvation given to us by God.

13–19 NOVEMBER   MATTHEW 11:1—12:50

1 **Soft robes and prophets** *Read Matthew 11:1–19*

Matthew now leaves the mission of the disciples and again focuses on the person of Jesus. In 8:27, after the stilling of the storm by Jesus, the disciples ask, 'What sort of man is this?' Here at the beginning of chapter 11, we find John the Baptist's disciples asking a very similar question concerning the identity of Jesus.

This section compares the old world order with the new represented by Jesus. We see the contrast between illness and wholeness, seeing and blindness, deafness and hearing. For those who can see and hear, the signs of the Kingdom are plain—wholeness has replaced illness, and death (whether physical or social) has been replaced with life.

Jesus asks the crowd what they expected to see when they went out to the wilderness where John was: grass or reeds, blown about by the wind? This is a powerful image: a modern-day equivalent would be to ask Christians if they went to their church only to count the bricks in the walls. It was John's fierceness, not his softness, which was his attraction to the crowds. Kings and wealth were a regular presence, but no stern, ascetic prophet had been seen for many years in Israel. For all their attraction to John, it seems that the crowds were not heeding his words.

Despite the accolade of greatness that Jesus bestows on John as prophet, he is still least in the Kingdom. He points the way to the Messiah and the coming Kingdom, and is the greatest in the old world order, but in the glorious new world to come, everything from the old world can only be inferior. John speaks from the threshold of the Kingdom, he represents the transition from the old to the new Kingdom of God. The time of fulfilment represented by Jesus outshines the era of promise many times. Yet despite this, the present generation cannot see the real roles of John and of Jesus. Like children, they are never satisfied with what is on offer and do not participate in the salvation offered by both John and Jesus. They chided John for his ascetic lifestyle. Jesus fares no better, being likened to a glutton and drunkard. John is too holy and Jesus is not holy enough, so how can they possibly claim to be sent by God? Like heavenly Wisdom, they will be rejected, but also like Wisdom, their righteous deeds will vindicate them.

2   Those whom Jesus calls   Read Matthew 11:20–30

Throughout this chapter, we have found Jesus confronted time and again with the disbelief of his compatriots. Despite the presence of God's messengers, and Jesus' ministry of healing and wholeness, many still remain blind and deaf to the message that Jesus brings. Jesus warns them again about the consequences of refusing to heed the truth.

Despite the hostility and resistance to his message, Jesus can still find the time to praise God. God is Lord of heaven and earth, and so it is God who remains in control of all the events, good and bad, that are happening around Jesus. Both those who accept the will of God and those who reject it are part of the outworking of the plan of God. Within this, people still have the freedom to choose to hear and follow the message of Jesus. Those who are receptive will receive the blessings that God's Kingdom promises to all who take up Jesus' challenge.

The prayer of Jesus in verses 25–27 can sound somewhat strange to our ears. It is an odd notion to thank God for hiding the truth from the wise and intelligent. But Jesus is making the point that it is the humble, the childlike and the lowly who are the most receptive, as their situations make them more dependent on the providence of God. The wise and intelligent can be deceived by their faith in their own cleverness. In this case, the idea of a humble Messiah announcing a spiritual kingdom is beyond the perception of the wise, who cannot see beyond the simple person of Jesus. Perhaps they were expecting a kingly and war-like Messiah to overthrow the Romans and restore Judea to the rule of its own people. It is clear that Jesus did not meet their expectations of Messiah.

Jesus invites all those who can see beyond his appearance to his real nature to enter into a relationship with him. He offers peace and rest to those who heed his call. The 'yoke' that Jesus refers to is a common theme found in Jewish writings. It symbolized the Law and obedience to God. Jesus offers the yoke of the Kingdom for those who have been oppressed and burdened by life. By being yoked to Jesus, the followers of Jesus, past and present, can share with him in the blessings of eternal life promised by God to the righteous.

3 Lord of the Sabbath *Read Matthew 12:1–14*

The Pharisees' previous criticisms of Jesus had been confined to questions to Jesus' disciples (9:10–11) or to conversation among themselves (9:3–4). Direct conflict with Jesus now occurs. They address him directly, and state why they think his actions and those of his disciples are unlawful. The conflict culminates in their departure in verse 14, when they go out to plan Jesus' destruction.

The Sabbath day was very important to Jewish people. It was the heart of their weekly religious life, where work would cease and God's goodness would be remembered and praised. The importance of observing the Sabbath was established in the Ten Commandments, and its observance was used by the prophets as a gauge of the nation's righteousness. It may be hard for us to understand exactly why the Pharisees in Matthew's Gospel thought that the disciples were acting unlawfully. The act of plucking the wheat, then removing the husk and chaff from the grain before eating it could well have been considered as harvesting the grain, work which was forbidden on the Sabbath. In true rabbinic style, Jesus debates with the Pharisees on this issue by using scriptural analogies, quotations and interpretation. He emphasizes that law without mercy cannot really be God's will, and concludes with the saying that the Son of Man is 'Lord of the Sabbath'. In the next scene we see a repetition of the conflict when Jesus heals the withered hand of a man on the same Sabbath day. The Pharisees fail to see the validity of Jesus' argument and leave to plot his downfall.

Concerned with the details of the religious argument, the Pharisees have failed to grasp the real meaning of Jesus' presence and action. Jesus, as God's Messiah, has the authority to decide and reveal what true observance of the Sabbath means. Matthew has already established this authority of Jesus in the Sermon on the Mount, where Jesus was revealed as the definitive interpreter of the Law. The Son of Man is also the Son of God, and as such is the final interpreter of the will of God as expressed by the Law and the Commandments.

The Pharisees sense that Jesus is a real threat to their religious system and structure. His removal is the only guarantee of its survival. It is their failure to accept Jesus as Messiah that leads to the tragedy of their becoming instruments in his death and destruction.

4 **Justice for Gentiles** *Read Matthew 12:15–21*

This is the second time that Matthew uses a scriptural quotation from Isaiah (Isaiah 42:1–3). Here Matthew explicitly spells out that Jesus is the servant of the Lord who will bring justice not only to Israel, but also to the Gentiles. Jesus represents the hope of salvation for all people. Here Matthew equates Jesus with the Servant motif found in what scholars often refer to as 'Second Isaiah' (Isaiah 40—55). Matthew has already claimed that Jesus is the light to the nations which penetrates the darkness (4:15–16). Here he is proclaimed as the bringer of justice to them. Further, Jesus is a servant of God who is quiet and unpretentious. His withdrawal from the plots of the Pharisees is not a sign of weakness or cowardice. He does not show his power ostentatiously or boast of his deeds. This Messiah is not the powerful and triumphant Messiah that was expected to restore Israel. Rather, the power of Jesus lay in his ability to bring to all people, Jew and Gentile, the grace of God's salvation.

At this point, Matthew appears to be borrowing not only verses from Second Isaiah, but some of the book's themes as well. The quoted verses appear in Isaiah in the context of God's offering comfort and the hope of a return home to the exiled people of Israel. The message of hope does not stop here, though. God goes on to offer universal salvation to the whole world. In the beginning of chapters 41, 42, 51 and 55 of Isaiah, God speaks of the nations that are expected to stream into Israel because they have seen the light of God's servant Israel. The nations are then to be judged by the servant of God.

Such an offer of salvation to the Gentiles is as unexpected as a Messiah who is humble and quiet. The Messiah was normally thought of as one who would bring justice to Israel and punishment to Israel's enemies. Jesus has come to reach out to those in most need—the poor, social outcasts, sinners and the downtrodden who are found among all nations. Today this truth can still catch us unawares. God is at work among all kinds of people. God's message of salvation and hope is not just for the righteous, but is available to all people of different classes and races.

5   A kingdom divided   *Read Matthew 12:22–37*

The conflict with the Pharisees continues. For the second time, they accuse Jesus of being in league with Beelzebul, ruler of the demons. Their reasoning seems to be along the lines that if Jesus himself is evil, then he will be able to order evil spirits what to do.

Jesus has just performed a miraculous healing of a blind, mute man. Matthew reports this event in one sentence. He does not dwell on the transformation of this man's life, or the joy it would have brought to him and his family. Instead, he gives this very brief account and moves to the real point of this section—the opposition of the Pharisees. The crowds are astonished, and wonder whether Jesus is the Son of David, the Messiah. The Pharisees see this as an impossible claim. They again seem to be incapable of understanding the true nature of the man who can perform such wonderful acts of restoration to wholeness. They fail to see how Jesus can possibly be the Messiah, the fulfilment of prophecy and the hope of the people. He must be the servant of the devil. The Pharisees' conclusion will cause the campaign against Jesus to gain momentum, and their ability to influence Jesus' fate will grow accordingly.

Jesus again responds to them with interpretive arguments, and also with a warning. He points out to them the foolishness of their argument, that a divided kingdom cannot stand strong. It must perish through civil war. All healings (or exorcisms) can only be the work of God, as they counteract the evil spirits and the work of the devil.

The Pharisees' charge of Jesus' consorting with the devil leads Jesus to speak of the 'unforgivable sin'. In their arrogance, they believe that they have divined the true secret of Jesus' power and named it as evil. This, says Jesus, is blasphemy against the Spirit, and cannot be forgiven. This statement by Jesus can only mean one thing: that his entire ministry depends upon the workings of the Holy Spirit, and it is the Spirit's presence that gives rise to his power and authority over illness, evil and the forces of nature. To reject the saving power of God, or to name it as evil, is an un-forgivable sin that directly denies God and the goodness and wholeness of being that will characterize the coming Kingdom.

6 Judgment and Jonah   *Read Matthew 12:38–50*

The Pharisees continue on their path of blindness. Having failed to understand the power of God when they see it, they now ask Jesus for a sign. This request reinforces their rejection of Jesus and his message. Despite witnessing many great miracles, the Pharisees still do not comprehend the true nature of what is before them. They have witnessed far more evidence than either the Ninevites or the Queen of Sheba had before them. With the very little information given to them by Jonah, the Ninevites had repented and turned to God. The Queen of Sheba had accepted the power of the Lord after merely meeting and conversing with the wise King Solomon. Yet despite the evidence they have witnessed of Jesus' power to heal and exorcise demons, the Pharisees can still ask for a further sign.

The sign to which Jesus refers them is rather cryptic, as it relates to his three days in the tomb before his resurrection. Further explanation is unnecessary. Jesus knows, as does the reader, that the Pharisees are going to reject this sign as well, and they will not change their minds about Jesus. The punishment for this lack of perception will be severe. At the close of the age, the Pharisees will find themselves a lot worse off than they are presently.

Jesus emphasizes how much worse their state will be by the use of a little parable about a demon who is cast out and then returns with many other demons to reinhabit the body. The final state of the possessed person is much worse than the original state. Jesus is concerned to point out that those who are privileged enough to be part of the time when the signs of the Kingdom of God are appearing among them should be the ones who can accept God's grace in a life-transforming and permanent way. Rejection of this grace is to invite back an evil much worse than that experienced initially, and to suffer worse miseries than previously experienced.

Jesus concludes his warnings by turning an everyday event—a request by his family to see him—into a further opportunity to emphasize the importance of following the will of the Father. Jesus' followers are his true family because they are obedient to his teaching. The Father of Jesus becomes the Father of all disciples, a new family centred on obedience to God shown by righteous behaviour.

GUIDELINES

There is nothing wrong in principle with desiring some sort of sign to confirm that something is truly from God. After all, personal experience of the grace of God helps us to nurture our faith. This is not true of Matthew's Pharisees. Throughout the last chapter, they have been presented with many signs which have provided good evidence that Jesus' power is from God. Their further request for a sign is therefore unjustified, as they have chosen to deny the reality of what Jesus stands for.

In the Pharisees' case, lack of faith and receptivity towards Jesus is the fundamental problem. It is unlikely that any sign would change their minds. They are determined to remain impermeable to the truth. In today's society, many sceptics still emulate the attitude of Matthew's Pharisees. Despite being presented with evidence of the truth of the gospel in a variety of ways, many choose to doubt its veracity. Others question its relevance to their lives, or suggest that Christianity has been a way of controlling the behaviour and opinions of too many people for too long, and should therefore be discarded like an outmoded and restrictive garment.

Those who challenge the truth of the gospel, or its power to heal and transform the lives of those who accept its message, are in no position to demand that wondrous signs be given as proof of its power. To ask for such evidence in these circumstances, to demand more signs and quantifiable evidence of God's existence, is to demonstrate a deep-seated lack of faith or belief in the reality of God and the grace that God offers. In this present age, we need the grace of God and the hope that comes from faith more than ever. We live in a fragile world in which evil is ever present and always looking for opportunities to assert its influence. We see its face in wars, escalating crime, oppression and environmental degradation.

To be part of the community of faith is to gain strength and hope from the conviction and faith of others. This allows us to resist the spread of evil. To be obedient to God gives us the means to fight actively against evil. As people of the Kingdom, we can increase the presence of God's Kingdom through our actions.

20–26 NOVEMBER   MATTHEW 13:1—14:34

1   The Kingdom and agriculture   *Read Matthew 13:1–23*

Many of the parables that Jesus tells in this Gospel are based on agricultural practices in the ancient world. In Jesus' time, most people produced their own food, so much of their day was spent in sowing, planting, weeding or harvesting their food crops. Only the wealthy would have been able to employ others to till their land or buy produce regularly at the markets. Jesus' parables, then, tell us something about the crowds that used to follow him around and listen to his words. Jesus does not speak often of buying or selling goods, but of growing crops, working the land and shepherding livestock. These were the daily pursuits of the poorer classes of people.

The section we read today contains one of Jesus' most well-known agricultural parables—the parable of the soils and the seeds, or the parable of the sower, as it is sometimes known. The story tells of a sower who 'went out' to sow seeds on various kinds of land. In his explanation of the parable to the disciples, Jesus makes it clear that he is the sower, his words are the seeds, and those who listen represent the different kinds of soil.

The sown words of Jesus have both complete failures and spectacular successes. Some people never really take in his message, and it is lost like the seed on the path. Others hear it, but forget when their faith is tested and the seed of the gospel withers away. Still others listen, and begin well, but find their faith 'choked' by worries or riches. Despite these losses, Jesus paints a picture of astonishing success for those who do hear and flourish in their faith. These seeds on the good soil bring forth an abundant harvest, which is described as a hundredfold and sixtyfold and thirtyfold. This crop is surely a spectacular success.

As Jesus the sower went out, so too today many other sowers continue to go out and spread the seeds of the gospel throughout the world. These sowers know that many things will destroy much of the seed they plant. Yet they still go out, year after year, and persist in the task of sharing the good news of Jesus. Their persistence in the face of many failures is not a testimony to their stubbornness or their stupidity, but a tribute to their faith and trust in God.

2 Wheat and weeds   *Read Matthew 13:24–30, 36–43*

Many of us love to look at or stroll around in a well-cared-for garden. We enjoy the flowers and appreciate the edible produce that is grown in gardens. Gardens involve a lot of hard work. They must be tended regularly. Despite this care, gardeners find themselves waging a constant battle against a common enemy of cultivated plants—the weed. Weeds are unwanted invaders in our garden. We deal with them by removing and destroying them. The parable we read today tells us that this battle with weeds is not new. Since humankind began cultivating land, weeds have been a constant enemy.

Weeds provide an excellent analogy for a parable of judgment.

They represent evil things that have no permanent place among useful or beautiful plants. They are to be destroyed lest they spoil the garden or harvest. This parable clearly tells a story about the fate of the godly and ungodly on earth at the end time. It looks straight-forward; but how can we tell who are the weeds and who are the wheat? If we imagine our society as a garden, who are the weeds in it?

A weed is really just an ordinary plant. It hasn't made a deliberate attack on our gardens; it is ensuring its survival as a plant. Some weeds even have many useful features, and can be used in cooking or as medicines. But at first glance, when compared to our cultivated plants, weeds appear ugly and superfluous. In the garden of today's societies, we often tend to think of the 'weeds' as the people who do not conform to our expectations of normal society. However, we cannot just uproot them as we do the weeds in our garden. We need to remember that, like the weeds in our garden, many of these people are not where they are by choice. Often they too are the victims of environment, chance factors and poor circumstances. They may be chronically unemployed or the victims of abuse and oppressive forces.

As Christians, how are we meant to deal with them? If we take the message of this parable at face value, it may seem that all we have to do is have faith ourselves, and not to worry about our societal weeds. However, the life of Jesus and much of his teaching call us to do much more. Jesus dealt with those who appeared to be the weeds of his society by loving them, teaching them, and not scorning them. His very presence on earth offered hope to misfits and sinners.

We need to remember that weeds grow profusely in gardens that are unloved or uncared for. In our society today, where many are increasingly alienated, oppressed or unloved, is it any wonder that the garden of our community has many who see themselves—wrongly—as useless weeds?

3 The kingdom of heaven is like…

Read Matthew 13:31–34, 44–53

Matthew places much emphasis throughout his Gospel on the coming of the kingdom of heaven (Matthew's preferred term for the kingdom, or reign, of God). This kingdom is eschatological (from the Greek *eschaton*, which means 'last') in nature; it has not yet arrived on earth, though signs telling of its coming are present in the ministry of Jesus. Admission to the kingdom is the reward for the followers of Jesus who are righteous and faithful to the will of God.

In this Gospel, Jesus often speaks about the nature and progress of the Kingdom of heaven, especially in the parables. In fact, in the midst of the six parables in our reading today we find the pronouncement that Jesus spoke to the crowd on this topic only in parables (v. 34). Matthew refers to the Kingdom of heaven over fifty times in his Gospel. There is an emphasis on the nearness of the Kingdom, which is described four times as having drawn near or come upon someone. When it comes, it will mean judgment for the righteous and unrighteous by the exalted Jesus, who states that this will occur in the lifetime of the disciples. Its coming will mark the end of the world as it is known and the beginning of the reign of God. Matthew's Jesus exhorts his followers to work actively for it and pray for its coming.

The Kingdom is expected to begin small and develop into something very large, and it is something worth giving up everything for. To tell people of its imminent arrival, the 'good news of the kingdom' is also to be proclaimed. The inheritors of the Kingdom, the righteous, have clearly defined ethical behaviour laid out for them to follow. More is required of them than mere faith in Jesus: they are exhorted to do and teach even the least of the commandments (5:19) and to do the will of the Father (7:21–23).

For Matthew, the kingdom is imminent, but not yet arrived; however, it is close enough for signs of its imminence to break into the present times as a demonstration and proof of its nearness (12:28). There is an urgency given to the proclamation of Jesus, who not only stresses that the kingdom of heaven is near, or at hand, but also implies that time is running out. The emphasis in the Gospel is not just on what the kingdom will be like, but on its imminence.

4 Grief and compassion *Read Matthew 13:54—14:21*

Chapter 13 ends with the rejection of Jesus by people from his home town. Believing that they know him and are familiar with him, they see only a carpenter's son who could not possibly know any more than they do. They reject his wisdom and his ministry. This rejection prepares us for the next chapter, where the agents of cynicism and unbelief react even more violently against Jesus and those who proclaim God's message.

Matthew has previously informed us of John the Baptist's arrest (4:12; 11:2) and now gives an account of his death. John had apparently proclaimed Herod to be an immoral man because he married his brother's wife, Herodias. Herod could see such a public denunciation only as treason, and John was arrested and put into prison. John's execution has been delayed, as Herod is afraid of the people. But the machinations of the wily Herodias lead to Herod's being tricked into agreeing to the execution. John's disciples bury his body and go to inform Jesus. By having Jesus withdraw by himself to a deserted place, Matthew suggests that Jesus is grieving for John and needs time alone. Perhaps even at this stage he is reflecting on his own death. But Jesus is denied his time of grief, because the crowds follow him from the towns around the lake.

Even when grieving, Jesus has compassion on the crowds and cures their sick. As evening approaches, the crowds are hungry. Jesus responds by producing much from little, a reflection of the growth of the Kingdom of God. The disciples' meagre provisions feed the whole crowd. Jesus has given a banquet in the wilderness from very little. This contrasts with Herod's birthday party, where the very few at his banquet had great abundance. It is this sort of selfish behaviour that leads to John the Baptist's death. Herod's selfish banquet and Jesus' joyous feast in the wilderness are contrasted. Herod's self-indulgence leads to his murder of God's prophet. Jesus' compassion leads him to satisfy the needs of the sick and hungry crowds.

John's death foreshadows that of Jesus, and the banquet Jesus holds is a foreshadowing of the heavenly banquet. The two together demonstrate some fundamental truths found in this Gospel. In John and Herod's case, it is better to be dead and live on in glory than to be physically alive and dead in spirit. Further, at the time of the heavenly banquet it is the least that will be present, not the great.

5 True religion *Read Matthew 14:22—15:20*

Today's reading is focused on the authority of Jesus, a favourite subject of Matthew's. It also looks at the ministry of the disciples, and foreshadows a time when Jesus will not be present with them.

Matthew presents these themes in a dramatic way. Jesus has gone alone to pray on a mountain, and the disciples are still in the boat on the lake. They are alone and drifting out on an increasingly stormy sea. Unable to land, they spend the night on the stormy waters. Early in the morning they see what they think is an apparition walking on the waves towards them. Jesus reassures them that it is he, and calls Peter to walk on his own across the water to Jesus. Peter becomes afraid, and has to be saved from sinking in the water. Jesus chides the disciples for their lack of faith. This story symbolizes the opposition that both Jesus and the disciples will meet. Their progress in preaching the gospel will be impeded by stormy times and opposition. When Jesus leaves the disciples alone to face the growing storm, they are afraid and panic. Their faith wavers and is not quite strong enough for them to cope alone. They do not perform well in this dress-rehearsal for their future mission, and are in danger of sinking amidst the turmoil. Peter stands as a prototype of the post-Easter Christians. He mixes fear and boldness, faith and doubt, obedience and confusion. He plays out the life of the infant Christian community in all its facets.

The symbolic turmoil and apparent opposition of the sea quickly become real at the beginning of chapter 15, where the Pharisees and scribes question the actions of Jesus and his disciples. In an argument about law and cleanliness, Jesus and the Pharisees are really defining boundaries regarding who belongs in the Kingdom and who is excluded. Jesus refuses to equate tradition with obedience to the will of God. Following traditions is not the same as doing the will of God, and there is always a risk that such traditions are self-serving. Selfishness cannot be concealed by a mere gloss of righteousness, despite the Pharisees' claim. Jesus emphasizes the point by calling them blind guides, who lead the people astray despite their pursuit of righteousness. Jesus concludes the argument by pointing out that it is hypocritical words and actions that defile, not unwashed hands. Only when the heart is clean can true righteousness be found.

6   The Canaanite woman   *Read Matthew 15:21–34*

In Matthew's Gospel, Jesus does not often meet and dialogue with non-Jewish people. Here he has withdrawn to the district of Tyre and Sidon. The Canaanite woman has come to seek him out—an indication that news of his marvellous deeds has spread to the regions outside of Israel, as the woman comes with the sole purpose of having her daughter healed.

This is a difficult passage to interpret, as the portrait painted by Matthew of Jesus is a rather harsh one. Unlike the account given by Mark, Matthew's Jesus initially ignores her request, and the disciples want her sent away. Her persistence leads to an initial rejection of her by Jesus, who states, 'I was sent only to the lost sheep of the house of Israel' (v. 24). Her request is rejected on the basis of her race: 'It is not fair to take the children's bread and throw it to the dogs' (v. 26). She responds to Jesus by pointing out that even dogs can catch crumbs that fall from the table. As a result of her clever interpretation of Jesus' remarks, he acknowledges her faith and grants her petition to heal her daughter.

What are we to make of Jesus' manners in this story? The woman belongs to a race that inspires Jewish scorn, labelled as being no better than a dog, and told that the Jews and their claims are superior to her own. Despite this, Jesus pronounces the faith of the Canaanite woman to be great. For all his impolite words to her, this believing Gentile woman can persuade him to share the benefits of the messianic age with her.

The faith of the Canaanite woman is contrasted with the religious practices of the Pharisees and scribes, which, according to Matthew, follow human teachings rather than divine. They are described as 'hypocrites' (15:7) and 'blind guides' (15:14), and it is inferred that they are of evil intent (15:19). Like the centurion of chapter 8, the Canaanite woman acts as a foil to the unbelief of the Jewish leaders, highlighting their failure to recognize the truth about Jesus.

The story is followed by an account of Jesus healing people from among the crowds who seek him out. Their response is to 'praise the God of Israel' (v. 31). The God of Israel is at work among all people.

Many of the passages we have read this week contain a number of Jesus' best-known stories and parables. It is likely that Jesus spoke in parables so that the peasant classes would clearly understand and accept the messages about God and faith that he wanted to convey to them. The parables allowed a largely agrarian class to hear the words of faith in familiar terms and concepts.

A problem we face today as we read these stories and parables is that they have become too familiar to us. They have been repeated to us many times in our life—in Sunday school lessons, sermons in church, and Bible reading guides such as this one. We are so sure of the storylines and accompanying explanations that the meaning no longer surprises us. The parables can be so familiar that sometimes we cease to hear them properly or to let them direct our faith in our daily lives. So we need to find ways of re-reading these familiar stories that open up the possibility of new interpretations. One way is to try to imagine how the crowds that followed Jesus around might have heard these stories for the first time.

Imagine for a moment that you are a farm worker back in first-century Palestine. You would be familiar with the hard work of harvesting the crops by hand. You would be alert to the possibility of excess rain or drought, or fights over the harvest by feuding village families. How might you hear the parable of the wheat and the weeds for the first time? Or that of the sower? Who would you envisage as the weeds? The seedlings that died when scorched? Would you see yourself or someone else in these roles?

Jesus clearly aimed his stories and parables at both sexes and different livelihoods. We find agriculture alongside merchant trading, and treasure hunting alongside leavened bread. Their variety makes them accessible to all people. Their familiarity and their unexpected elements reassure and challenge us simultaneously. These simple stories reveal to us what God is doing in the world through the ministry of Jesus, both today and long ago. They still have the power to help us to choose our path wisely from among the many choices we are faced with each day.

Last week we read many of the parables and stories of Jesus, and looked for fresh ways to view them. In this week's readings, we come to one of the high points of Matthew's Gospel, the great confession of Peter. As well as being a moment of great discernment on the part of the disciples, it also becomes a time of dismay and soul-searching, as Jesus reveals his true destiny for the first time.

1   The leaven of the Pharisees   Read Matthew 16:1–12

The Pharisees, this time accompanied by the Sadducees, again want to harangue Jesus. They come to him, not for healing as the crowds do, but to test him. They demand a sign, some indication from heaven to indicate that Jesus speaks the truth. They are obviously suspicious of Jesus' power and the claims he has made.

The question that may have been uppermost in the minds of the Pharisees and Sadducees is whether or not God approved of this man Jesus. After all, proof of such approval would require a serious rethink of their attitudes, a hard task indeed. It is also possible that they secretly feared that the crowds surrounding him were the first sign of a revolt against Rome, the ruling power. Though the Pharisees certainly did not approve of Roman domination, a revolutionary among the Jewish people could only lead to trouble. Because of such a fear, they may have intended to entrap Jesus into giving an answer that they could use against him in a report to the authorities.

Whatever their reason, Jesus responds to them with a rebuke. He notes that they can predict the weather by reading the sky, the face of the heavens, yet cannot access heaven to read the sign of the times. They can interpret sunrises and sunsets, but cannot interpret Jesus' words and deeds. Thus their righteousness is deceptive, based on their own rather than God's authority. Jesus therefore takes the opportunity to warn his disciples against the leaven of the Pharisees and Sadducees. It is important for them to understand that, as representatives of the truth, they will face opposition from these groups.

The next part that follows is almost like a comic skit. Matthew obviously needs a bunch of blockheads to allow for an opportunity to teach the truth. So inevitably the disciples take the reference to leaven literally, and acknowledge that they have no bread. The disciples fail to benefit from their recent experience of the miraculous feast. They cannot see that Jesus feeds their hunger and thirst not in a literal sense, but spiritually. Jesus' teaching is itself the sustenance of eternal life, solid and dependable. The description of the Pharisees' teaching as leaven is perhaps the ancient Jewish way of describing something as 'hot air' and, as such, very unsatisfying. Those who seek the truth will be satisfied by Jesus' bread, and filled with new and sustaining life.

2   The rock and the church   *Read Matthew 16:13–27*

In our Christian life today, we usually take the fact of Jesus' Messiahship for granted. We have grown up being taught that Jesus is God's Son. We take it as read that Jesus is the definitive revelation of the Father to us in a way we can clearly understand.

Let us imagine for a moment how the disciples viewed Jesus up until this point. He was someone special, but still a lot like them. He had a trade and a family just like them, though clearly his scriptural wisdom was greater. But was he the Messiah? Jesus certainly hadn't claimed the *title* for himself. Such a step of faith in him would have been a large one. Now in the Gospel, we find the disciples ready to take it.

The question 'Who is this man?' has already been asked by the disciples (e.g. 8:27). In this section, Jesus himself asks, 'Who do people say I am?' The disciples report that there are a number of views as to Jesus' identity. Jesus then queries who the disciples think he is. Here for the first time, a human character, Simon— who recognizes that Jesus is in fact the *Christos*, the Messiah— names Jesus' full identity. Simon is declared by Jesus to be 'blessed' for his confession. He is also given a new name: 'Peter' (*Petros* in Greek) is the 'rock' on which the foundations of the 'church' will be built. Despite his new name, however, Peter does not display solid or rock-like qualities. Within a few verses, Jesus will roundly scold him for his failure to understand God's purpose: he is therefore a 'rock' who causes others to stumble. Yet who can fail to sympathize with Peter? Like most of us, he is a mixture of discernment and ignorance, success and failure. Yet it is the likes of Peter who will give a firm foundation to the new community of faith, the Church.

The use of the word 'church' is unique to this Gospel. It suggests that Matthew is writing at a time when his Christian community is keen to establish its identity. So in this passage, the question of the identity of Jesus is not just about Jesus, but also about his followers. These followers are called by Jesus to take up their cross and follow him along the path of martyrdom to ultimate glory. This must have been another shock to the disciples. Having redefined their view of Jesus, they now need to redefine their own role. It was probably as hard for them as it is for us to grasp the paradox of discipleship. To give up one's life (literally or figuratively) in the service of God is truly to find it.

3 **Depths and heights**   *Read Matthew 17:1–23*

Our last few readings have highlighted how the faith of the disciples swung between belief and doubt, understanding and ignorance. This pendulum-swing between contrasting states continues into chapter 17. We ascend the mountain with three disciples and Jesus to where his transfiguration takes place. We descend with them to find that the remaining nine disciples at the bottom of the mountain are unable to exorcise a demon from an epileptic boy. On the mountain, Jesus touches and reassures the three disciples gently. At the foot of the mountain, the nine are chastised for their lack of faith. By the end of the section, all the disciples are greatly distressed when Jesus again announces the details of his fate.

The new scene opens well. On the mountain, the disciples witness Jesus transformed in a way that equates him with the greatest of lawgivers (Moses) and the greatest of the prophets (Elijah). The message is clear: Jesus is the new lawgiver, as well as the supreme prophetic teacher. At the height of the transcendent scene, the divine voice says of Jesus, 'Listen to him!' What an experience this must have been for the three disciples! Having heard Jesus speak only a few days before in a most unexpected way about his death being part of the divine plan, here they are given some reassurance that death is only part of the plan for

God's Messiah, for death will be followed by resurrection. The role that Jesus has to play in God's plan is pivotal. As 'Elijah', John the Baptizer has prepared the way for Jesus; now Jesus (as the Messiah who follows after Elijah) will execute God's purposes in full.

The reassurance that Jesus offers does not come without a price, however. Jesus gives the command to listen a terrible poignancy, for to follow his teaching is to follow the narrow path of suffering. Naturally, this causes the disciples much distress. How ironic, then, that alongside this moment of great revelation of the significance of Jesus, the disciples plumb the depths of despair. Yet life as we know it is often marked by this complexity of highs and lows side by side.

Jesus' person and teaching are established as the authority that God commands all to listen to. To follow him means to be prepared for suffering and even death. We can be reassured, however, that this is all integral to the plan of God. Jesus leads us to God and enables us to be God's people in the world.

4   Temples, taxes and authority
Read Matthew 17:24–27; 22:15–22

One of the proverbs that we most often hear quoted concerns the certainty of death and taxes. Even in ancient times, taxes were one of the facts of life. The Messiah—and his disciples—are not exempt. In these two sections, we again meet Peter in dialogue with Jesus. However, this time it is not to discuss faith or lack of it, but the more mundane issue of paying taxes.

Jews living in the Palestine area before the destruction of the temple in AD70 had an obligation to pay at least two types of taxes. The first, mentioned in chapter 17, was known as the 'temple tax'. This may have been based on the levy mentioned in Exodus 30:11–16; or it may have been an additional Roman tax imposed on Jewish people. The second, referred to in chapter 22, was the tax that all residents in the Roman empire had to pay direct to the Roman administrators.

In the first passage, we have two short scenes. Peter is asked initially by certain tax collectors in Capernaum whether Jesus pays the temple tax. He answers, 'Yes.' In the second scene, Peter goes to Jesus and is instructed about the temple tax and how to pay it—though it must be said that Jesus' way of paying tax was highly unusual! In the second excerpt, Jesus must easily have worked out that the question he was asked was a trap. After all, when two traditional enemies join forces to question you, it is reasonable to assume that trouble will shortly follow. We know from our previous readings that the Pharisees saw Jesus as a troublesome blasphemer, though they did not support the Roman overlords. The other group, the Herodians, did support the client kings of the Romans. Jesus is confronted by the two groups who will damn him for saying 'yes' or 'no'. He would confirm that he is either a blasphemer by a 'yes' or a revolutionary by a 'no'. Jesus foils their plot by showing a third way. He gives what is due to both God and Caesar. He neither collaborates with, nor speaks violently against, the Roman oppressor. As such, Jesus transcends the dilemma of the trap laid for him.

Jesus was not a revolutionary who set out to win people to his cause by championing political freedom for Israel. He concedes that there is a restricted duty owed to the government, but balances this with the more important command to give God what is God's. Jesus teaches that it is our very selves we render to God, not a token amount of money.

5   Forgiveness and reconciliation   *Read Matthew 18:1–14*

The chapter opens with a question from the disciples: 'Who is the greatest in the kingdom of heaven?' Perhaps they had been reflecting on this question at length. Perhaps they thought that as their knowledge and understanding of Jesus' teaching was greater than that of the common folk who followed him, they would be given authority over others in God's new Kingdom. If this is the way they were thinking, then they were doomed to disappoint- ment. Jesus quickly dispels any such notions by his answer. He again demonstrates the paradox of faith: the least are, in fact, the greatest.

In Palestine, children did not hold positions of prominence. Most unexpectedly, Jesus regards children as role models for faith and greatness. The disciples must have been surprised at this stance, as they seemed to have quite an opposite view of greatness —as power and pride of position. The saying that whoever welcomes a child welcomes Jesus is a brief word which foreshadows the more detailed teaching along these lines in the parable of the sheep and the goats (Matthew 25:31–46), where the care for 'the least of my brothers and sisters' equals care for Jesus himself.

It has long been recognized by biblical scholars that the term 'little ones' is a cryptic way in which Matthew refers to disciples of Jesus. Particular instructions concerning the 'little ones' are found in verses 6–9 and contain some of the 'hard sayings' of Jesus that the Church has tended to ignore or overlook. Jesus teaches that these believers in Jesus are so important that to receive them is to receive Jesus himself. To hinder them is to risk punishment from God. In fact, these believers are so important that Jesus, the shepherd, will leave the other sheep to search for one lost one— not a practical way for a real shepherd to behave, perhaps, but a clear demonstration of the infinite love Jesus holds for all who follow him. The words are not just directed to those outside the community, though. They contain an indirect warning to believers to avoid things in their own lives that may cause them to stumble and affect their life in the Kingdom.

Jesus' intense words warn would-be disciples that they must be known by their humility, and stand apart from a world obsessed with status and material values. Living this way ensures the survival of the church community, as each believer is expected to love and respect every other believer in the same way that God loves them.

6   If your brother or sister sins   *Read Matthew 18:14–35*

Jesus' words here are more than just advice to the disciples. The Gospel stresses that his words and life are also a guidebook for those who are part of a Christian community.

Jesus gives some helpful examples of how Christian communities can live in harmony and find ways of dealing with grievances among their members. Procedures are outlined that make Christians accountable to their community, with recalcitrants dealt with by ostracism. In Matthew's time, this was a very serious thing: to be rejected by the Christian community meant that Christianity was no longer a genuine option, as Christians were few and often isolated. Today's Christian communities are rather different. A member can leave one denomination and walk down the road to another church. Nevertheless, the guidelines set down here still have a lot to teach us, especially with regard to the process and necessity of forgiveness.

Jesus stresses that all possible means must be tried to resolve the dispute, and he clearly defines what steps must be taken. The two parties should first try to resolve the dispute among themselves. If this fails, then the matter is to be discussed again in the presence of a few others in the community. The next step is to be guided by the church community. If this fails, then ostracism is the final resort. A vital part of this process is forgiveness, a quality that is modelled on the mercy and grace of God's free forgiveness of sin. Jesus emphasizes this necessary quality of discipleship in the parable of the unforgiving servant. The parable underscores the notion that God forgives those who themselves show mercy. The failure to forgive another who has wronged us has very serious consequences. Not only is the unforgiving person cut off from the community, but he or she is also cut off from the love and mercy of God.

The Christian community must treat its members as God treats them. Failure to forgive is a failure to embody the Kingdom of God and, ultimately, a failure to be the body of Christ.

GUIDELINES

In much of the previous chapter, Jesus has laid down guidelines and rules regarding how his followers in a Christian community might function. The central issues are those of humility, service and forgiveness. Implicit is the notion that there is no hierarchy, that all are equal within the group that follows Jesus. The simple principle that undergirds the workings of the community is not the obedience of the lesser to the greater (except, of course, when the greater is God!) but forgiveness of one another as each tries to live out their faith in community.

It is a sad indictment on many modern Christian faith communities that this basic principle is rarely put into practice. Jesus speaks of resolving disputes initially by a confidential discussion between those concerned, then with a few others aware of the situation, and then a public meeting with the whole church. More often than not in our churches today, the discussion of such issues is conducted via gossip and thus through a series of inter-mediaries. Such methods result in much hurt, misunderstanding and anger. The dispute is supposedly resolved either by sweeping the matter under the carpet, or by one or more of those involved leaving the church. Jesus tells us to be forgiving rather than vengeful, and direct in our dealings with each other rather than be-coming gossips. His directions are very plain, yet we seem to have endless difficulty in following them.

It is impossible to be in relationship with God if we cannot be in relationship with one another. We cannot be sincere in our worship unless we are sincere in doing the will of God. We need to cultivate attitudes of acceptance and understanding, which in turn can lead to forgiveness. We can reject gossip for honest dis-cussion. We can help others to feel that we are listening to them and prepared to walk alongside them. It is in supporting each other in love that we truly become the body of Christ.

Further reading

In addition to the works listed at the end of the last issue of Guidelines, see:

M. Davies, *Matthew*, JSOT, 1993.

J.C. Fenton, *The Gospel of St Matthew*, Penguin, 1963.

R.H. Smith, *Matthew*, Augsburg, 1989.

G. Stanton, *A Gospel for a New People: Studies in Matthew*, T&T Clark, 1992.

Psalms for Advent:
waiting for the Lord

We are not very good at waiting for Christmas, for that solemn night and morning that commemorate the birth of our Saviour, the Word made flesh. We cannot wait so long. So our 'Christmas' is, in effect, brought further and further forward, as some use it to boost trade, others suit their convenience, and most anyway find waiting irksome.

But the season of Advent should be a time of waiting, a waiting that is by no means barren. To help us to explore the several aspects of this fruitful vigil, we shall be following the theme of waiting for the Lord in a selection of psalm passages. There is not just one Hebrew word for 'waiting', but a number of expressions which, as the passages show, range over the experiences that may be involved in waiting and watching for the Lord.

Thus we shall meet the distress of long suffering, and also the stillness that acknowledges the sovereignty of the Lord. We shall meet the sufferers whose faith makes them confident and ready to give thanks for the help that will surely come. There will also be a waiting in quiet awe in the powerful presence of God, and a waiting that is a journey in hope, when the knowledge of what God will do lightens the step and cheers the heart through many weary miles. We shall hear the prayer of the waiting ones, as they plead with their Lord to come soon, and again and again we shall see how waiting is transformed by being directed to the Lord. We shall see how waiting was supported by trust and expectancy. A time of peacefulness will be found, when querulous fears have been stilled in love. And we shall meet those who watch through the nights to bless the Lord, and in the darkness take blessing from him, for themselves and for the heaven and earth that he has made.

It may be that we shall readily identify with some of the psalmists who wait for the Lord. Our present circumstances may parallel theirs. But the psalms also call us to a representative work. As we read and pray these ancient psalms of waiting, we wait also on behalf of all who watch through the night of trial. In the sympathy of the Holy Spirit, we fix our eyes on the Lord, until he has mercy on all his creatures.

No particular translation is used in these notes. Direct quotations are rendered straight from the Hebrew.

4–10 DECEMBER   VERSES FROM PSALMS 33–65

1   The essence of the waiting   *Read Psalm 33:16–22*

The heart of what it means to wait upon the Lord is soon apparent in our passage. Those who wait and watch for him have awareness of his reality as God, maker and governor of all, the one true Saviour. In lands where invasion and conquest were all too common, it was easy to think of military might as decisive. The strong and well-armed warriors, the vast array of chariots and warhorses—such forces of great kings might well seem to be the real powers on earth. But our psalm insists that they in themselves are powerless to save. Salvation is from the Lord alone, and his caring eye is especially on those who 'fear' him, those who live day by day in keen awareness of his supreme power and reality, waiting in confidence for his faithful love.

So the psalm leads us to aspire to a trustful waiting for him, our true help and shield (v. 20). We look forward to the joy of his salvation, for we have put our trust in his holy name (v. 21). In his name, he himself comes to us, makes himself known, and invites us to talk and walk with him.

The conclusion is a prayer: 'May your faithful love be upon us, O Lord, as we have waited for you.' The goodness of the Lord is known especially to the expectant soul; and for one who believes, all things are possible. But from 'death' and 'famine' (v. 19) will he always deliver those who fear him and wait for his sure love? It is hard to affirm this flatly, until we can see beyond this life. But already we may learn in our own experience that, as we wait upon him, we are freed from a withering, a leanness in our soul. As we wait upon him and trust in his holy name, true life courses in us: 'our heart shall rejoice in him'.

2 The long wait in suffering *Read Psalm 40:1–5*

This part of Psalm 40 is a kind of introduction, a preparation for the prayer of verses 11–17. In a time of need, the one who prays begins here by recalling a past deliverance. It was a wonderful work of God which opened the eyes to the sheer multitude of his mercies, influenced others to have faith, and renewed the one who was saved in total dedication to the service of God. Perhaps all this is recalled to stir courage and faith for the new prayer that has to be made in the new situation of need. But there is a childlike quality in biblical prayer, and these verses of introduction and preparation may also be intended to move the Lord's own compassion. May God remember that great past deliverance, and the praise, witness and faith that flowed from it, and may he hear and answer now!

Looking at some of the details in this recollection of earlier salvation, we note especially the long ordeal of waiting. The opening is commonly translated, 'I waited patiently for the Lord'. The Hebrew, however, does not specify 'patiently'. but indicates a waiting that went to the extreme; it may indeed refer to loud prayers of distress. There was a long time of apparent forsakenness, until the turn to salvation came, until the Lord 'inclined to me and heard my crying'.

Nor was it a waiting in a still and silent place. It was in a dreadful place of tumult, as it were (for the Hebrew imagination) in the mouth of the great cavern of Death, where chaotic waves thundered together and the sufferer's feet sank in bottomless mire.

But the Lord proved true: 'He set my feet upon a rock'. Sweet was that hour of salvation, and sweet the song of gratitude that filled the heart. The song flowed out in testimony, and many that heard it learned to trust in the Lord and found the happiness of life in that trust, so different from the fraud of arrogant ways. That act of rescue opened many eyes to the marvels of God that are all around, the infinite work of the One who has no equal.

From these verses, then, we hear of a waiting that was long and terrible, but which held on into—almost beyond—the extremes, till the Rock was found and the song of joy was given. As now we wait for Christ, we cannot but think of how he suffered in the mouth of Death, so that multitudes might fear and believe and be saved. That recollection will suffice as a preparation and under-girding of all our prayer in present need.

3 A counsel of stillness for the nations *Read Psalm 46:8–11*

In the course of this great psalm, a terrible prospect is revealed—the world thrown into chaos, a tumult of cosmic disorder and violent nations. Yet through it all is seen the God who can master the chaos, saving his holy city and people at the break of morning and vindicating their trust in him.

It may well be that these visionary thoughts arose from cere-monies of worship in the festal season of (autumnal) New Year and Tabernacles. Words and actions in such ceremonies amounted to a great poem or vision. It interpreted the tragedies and hopes of life, and brought the enraptured people a fresh sense of God's reign over all.

The psalm invites us to share the vision. Come and see what destruction God has wrought across the earth—but a good des-truction, shattering the cruel weapons of war! See the good Kingdom beyond this time of tumult! And the sense of God revealed in majesty leads the singer to voice God's words (v. 10): 'Be still, and know...' These haunting words, we see, were not first meant as comfort for an individual. Rather the message was a warning to greedy and cruel nations. They are to desist from their turbulent and selfish deeds and realize where true power lies. They are to reckon with the awesome God.

So here is a waiting, a stillness, enjoined upon the peoples and power-blocks of the world. The Church also, in continuance of the Bible's way, should not hesitate to address whole peoples and their rulers. They must ever and again be warned not to be God to themselves, as though they had none to answer to.

4 A heart ready to praise *Read Psalm 57:7–11*

The psalm headings are of mixed value. The more ancient parts are often obscure, while some additions (in this case 'when he fled from Saul in the cave') may represent a later interpretation. Nevertheless, we can agree so far with the heading that this psalm was the prayer of a king, a solemn intercession for the preservation of the nation. Through the night of prayer, his soul has sought refuge in the Lord, to shelter under his wings from monstrous foes. The dangers are not defined—only that the foes are like fire-breathing lions, deadly in teeth and tongue.

Our passage expresses rising hope as night draws to an end. The king's heart is ready to praise God, offering to him the melody of psalm music. He calls to his soul ('my glory') and to the harp and lyre that were the usual accompaniment of psalm singing; he calls to them to awake, that together they may awaken the dawn. Here he echoes the very ancient thought that the morning praise of temples called heaven and earth to awake and rejoice in the beauty of God. His own song will especially testify to the faithfulness of the Lord, the love that keeps to its pledge. To all peoples he will testify that this love is great beyond all telling, reaching as it were from earth to the clouds and the very heavens.

Can the Lord disappoint such a willing witness to his faithfulness? The childlike thought seems to prompt our passage. Approach of morning has not banished all danger and trouble, but the night of prayer has indeed reached its most pressing force with this culmination in anticipatory thankfulness. The closing verse resumes the essential prayer from verse 5: may God arise in open power, dispelling with his glory the forces of darkness!

Even in the midst of our distresses, we too can be ready to give thanks and testimony. With our waiting heart set and prepared for the song in praise of God's faithful love, we are on the verge of the turn to morning. We shall awaken our soul to its depths, and even play our part in awakening the dawn. For the one who makes music to God and sings of his love among the peoples is helping to bring in the light of God.

5   A soul still and expectant   *Read Psalm 62:1–8*

A soul still before God, waiting in quietness and trust—what an idyllic scene of tranquillity! But we soon see in this passage that such stillness defies the circumstances. This person of 'eminence' (v. 4), probably a king, is the focus of much hostility. Called to be a defence for his people, he feels like a wall battered by siege-engines and near to collapse (v. 3). The assaults are all the worse for being planned and done with deceit and hypocrisy.

He and his people may be tempted to think that the ways of the ruthless are the ways that succeed; wealth and power easily seem to be the reward of the unscrupulous. Against this temptation, and ever in much peril, the psalmist urges his people and his own soul to realize afresh that God is the only strength and salvation. The stillness to God (vv. 1, 5) is a quiet waiting before him in trust and hope, acknowledging that all power belongs to him, the faithful and compassionate Lord of all. The rich phrases of trust were traditional in the prayers of the Davidic kings, in constant danger but appealing to the ancient promises of God: 'my rock, my salvation, my high tower, my glory, the rock of my strength, my refuge'. These promises to the Lord's anointed gave shelter also to all his loyal people, and he calls on them also to trust in God at all times and to pour out their heart before him (v. 8). This 'pouring out' is a placing of all one's inner being like a sacrifice before God's altar—one's weakness and fear, one's grief and hope. All is poured out before him, and then in the stillness he fills our emptiness with his grace. We know him as our refuge and our glory.

6 Hushed in adoration   *Read Psalm 65:1–8*

The opening words surprise translators and divide them. Some offer the banal thought that praise 'is fitting' for God in Zion, and some even state that praise 'is due'. On reflection, however, the plain sense of the Hebrew seems good. The praise is 'silence', so: 'Praise is hushed for you, O God, in Zion, and vows shall be paid to you that answer prayer'. It is the dramatic moment in the great festival in Jerusalem when the awesome presence of God dominates the minds of the massed worshippers in the open court. The Lord is present and ready to receive the offerings vowed in the crises of the foregoing year. It is the moment when the cry would go forth: 'Be silent at the presence of the Lord God' (Zephaniah 1:7); 'Let all the earth keep silence before him' (Habakkuk 2:20). It is the time when the best praise is silence, a waiting in stillness before the Lord in his greatness.

Then comes the recollection of help he has given in recent times—all his answering of prayers. The offerings now to be made in thanksgiving are, above all, an acknowledgment of his grace and a testimony to others. And of all his works of rescue, the greatest is his overcoming of sins. They are too many and strong for us, but he can cleanse us and enable us to enter his presence. Through that work of grace, we can 'dwell in his courts', and be replenished by 'the goodness of his house', life in communion with him.

The worshippers were gathered, no doubt, for New Year and Tabernacles, when the cycle of the year began afresh in autumn. Most were subsistence farmers, and a bad year would bring much starvation and bondage. The psalm, then, encourages faith in the good Lord's power over the great natural forces. What wonders he did in establishing the order of life! Faith sees him continuing to prepare and bestow all that will be needed in the days to come (vv. 9–13 being best taken as prayer and hope for the coming year).

Our psalm reflects the profound thoughts of worshippers who know that life and existence hang on the mercy of God. And all the homage and prayer have begun with a hushed waiting before this holy Creator—the praise of silence.

Watch thou, dear Lord, with those who wake, or watch, or weep tonight, and give thine angels charge over those who sleep. Tend thy sick ones, O Lord Christ; rest thy weary ones; shield thy joyous ones; and all for thy love's sake.

A prayer of St Augustine

11–17 DECEMBER   VERSES FROM PSALMS 84—134

1   The pilgrim's hope   *Read Psalm 84:1–7*

The psalm, in part, sings of the longing and hope of those who made pilgrimage to God's powerful and gracious presence in Jerusalem. Its thoughts and images can readily be applied to our whole life as a pilgrimage, but also to our journey through Advent. For in Advent we may journey in spirit with longing and hope to reach at last the manger and the Word made flesh.

The psalm opens with an exclamation: how lovely and how greatly loved is the dwelling place of the almighty Lord! From the standpoint of one who has found this holy place, the singer then looks back (so the Hebrew is best taken) to the days of pilgrimage, when the soul fainted with longing for the courts of the Lord, and heart and flesh cried out in need for the source of life, 'the living God'. The beautiful image of verse 3 then refers to the joy and contentment of having reached the goal of the pilgrimage: as a swallow might nest in the walls or roofs near the altar in the great court, so the longing soul finds her true home in the presence of God.

How happy those who dwell here always and offer praise continually! So verse 4, referring to those who serve at the temple. But happy too (vv. 5–7) those who come as pilgrims! Already on their journey, they draw strength from God, for their hope and their aim are towards him. In their heart are the 'highways', or rather, the sacred way that leads up to his temple; their imagination and desire are set on that joyful ascent to the Lord, when the hardships and dangers of the journey will have been passed through.

Before that happy fulfilment, the pilgrims pass through a valley of harsh dryness, but where their feet have trodden (so was the old belief) the longed-for rains will fall, covering the ground with the blessing of life. They struggle over arid ground and, beyond their knowing, they have made it a place of springs; not immediately, but in God's good time, his life and grace will abound there. Their weariness may appear to increase, but as every step brings them nearer their home in God, their spirit in reality goes from strength to strength.

The pilgrimage is readily seen as a model of life's journey. But, on a smaller scale, it is also a model for Advent. Following the star of faith, we pass through weeks of special prayer, watching with many a sufferer and longing for fuller sight of Christ, until we come to Bethlehem. Who knows what springs of blessing our footsteps, in God's time, may bring to the thirsty ground?

2   Oh when will you come to me?   *Read Psalm 101*

An ideal is expressed in this psalm—that of a king who is devoted to the Lord in worship and in the government of his city and society. He does not allow corrupt ministers to have a place in his government, and morning by morning, in judicial sittings, he upholds justice for the poor and roots out oppressors.

The opening has caused some difficulty. We can translate: 'Of faithful love and justice will I sing; to you, O Lord, I raise my psalm. My song shall be of the way that is pure—oh when will you come to me?' It is thus clear that the psalm is an impassioned plea raised to the Lord. From a situation of need, when God seems far off, the king pleads his loyalty and integrity (or his promise of these) in supplication that the Lord will come to him with salvation. It is quite possible that the scene is from dramatic ceremonies of royal installation, where the rite would have shown the king's utter dependence on a God who requires just dealing.

As we in our turn look for the Lord to come to us with salvation, we also must give heed to the way that is pure. Advent, like Lent, should be a time to examine our ways in home, workplace, and out and about. The psalm would have us especially abhor dishonest and devious schemes, deeds of unfaithfulness, slander, arrogance, greed and deceit. If we truly desire and endeavour to keep the kingdom that is our own heart pure and free from such false things, then we too can raise to the Lord our hopes and longing: 'Oh come to us, be born in us, our Lord Immanuel!'

The psalm is indeed a song of the 'faithful love and justice' which God requires of his king, but these opening words seem also to echo the thought so often expressed in the psalms that God himself deals with his world and his people with 'faithful love' (Hebrew *hesed*). Down the centuries, this word in a great many passages was rendered 'mercy', and when we face up to God's laws of conduct, it is his mercy above all that sustains us. His compassionate love is the ground of our hope; yet our longing for him should be also a longing for what pleases him—a pure and humble heart.

3   Sheltered in the circle of the mountains   *Read Psalm 125*

Our remaining readings are all from psalms headed 'Song of ascents (or steps)'. It is not clear whether we should think of songs for the 'going up' to Jerusalem, or for use on the final 'steps' or 'stairs' of the sacred way. In any case, it is an especially beautiful group of songs, gladdening those who go up to God, the source of life.

Our passages about 'waiting for the Lord' are often interwoven with the theme of trusting in him. We wait for him with deep trust that he, in his power and love, is sufficient for all our needs. Such trust, according to our present reading, places us in the circle of

God's protection, just as the holy city was ringed by a circle of protecting mountains.

But our psalm does not make its testimony from easy circumstances. The 'sceptre of wickedness', an evil dominion, seems at present to overshadow the society, and within society there are those who 'turn aside to crooked ways'. So prayer is raised that the Lord will do good to those who are good and true of heart. It is evidently one of those situations where it seems that the good must suffer, while the crooked ones have not received their deserts. The psalm's last word, then, is with prayer: may peace, the wholeness of blessing, be upon the true people of God!

History was in fact to show that Mount Zion, the temple and the holy city, were not safe in their circle of mountains. Invasion and destruction came, and came again. The protection was relative, and did afford precious centuries when the the holy city's role could be developed and made for ever fruitful. And perhaps there is an insight here for us. Times of evident peace and security are given for purposes of God, for the rooting and growing of his work in and through us. But there will also be times of danger and turmoil, times when evil dominion and crooked ways seem to prevail all about us. In such times of suffering, the encircling protection of God is a mystery. So it was in our Lord's passion, and for many of his loyal followers. It is a mystery—not comprehensible as we should wish, but there to be discovered as real and true beyond all the passing shadows of this earthly life.

4   Watching for the dawn   *Read Psalm 130*

The one who utters this cry of supplication to the Lord seems to pray as representative for the people (note vv. 7–8). It is a time when all their sufferings and failures are brought before the Lord, perhaps the vigil before the annual ceremonies of penitence and atonement. 'From the depths', from the very jaws of destruction and final darkness, the cry rises to the merciful Lord. It is not his will to 'keep' offences, retaining the record against his failing people. With him there is forgiveness. He forgives that he may be 'feared'—that he may have a renewed people, devout and alive to his reality and presence.

The singer tells of a most eager and earnest 'waiting' for the

Lord. Heart and soul look for his reconciling 'word', indeed for the Lord himself, as eagerly as watchmen watch for the first signs of morning. The comparison may be with the priestly watchers, high on the walls, whose duty it was to give the signal for the morning offering in the temple. Turning then to the people, the psalmist urges them so to wait and watch for the Lord, in sure hope of his faithful love and overflowing will to redeem.

In the depths of our own sufferings and failures, and in sympathy also with all the sorrowful and fallen of the world, the psalm would have us look to the Lord, waiting and watching for his approaching light, mindful of his forgiveness, his abundant redemption, and his love that never turns us away.

5 The quieted child   *Read Psalm 131*

Here is a waiting which makes appeal to the Lord by its very restraint. The singer turns to the Lord not with heart and eyes raised high, as though able to argue with God on an equal footing, bold to tell him what he should be doing. Rather he acknowledges that God's work is great and wonderful beyond human understanding. There has been much for him and his people to endure, and his soul might well have raised clamour and protest, but he has restrained and quieted it.

The singer compares this quieting to the task of a mother who weans her child. The change from breast-feeding disturbs the child, which struggles and cries in frustration. She soothes and calms it, until at last the transition is completed, and her child rests peacefully again in her arms. 'I have quieted and stilled my soul,' says the psalmist, 'as a weaned child upon its mother; so my soul is quieted on me.'

And this itself is a quiet way of appealing to the Lord. The sufferings he might have shouted about are still there, but he says in effect, 'You know them all, Lord, and alone know how to deal with them. I trust you and I wait for you in quiet hope.' And to the people worshipping with him he finally turns, and he calls on them in the same spirit to wait for the Lord.

The psalm makes us wonder again at the richness of what the Bible shows about prayer and the walk with God. Often it is the frankness that strikes us—the bold, almost strident crying out to

God, the outspokenness of a grieving child. But then again, as our reading has shown, there is a different mood, where humility and childlike trust prevail in a calmed 'waiting unto the Lord'. For both moods, comparison with a child has come to mind, and here is the key to the biblical way of prayer—turning to the God who is our mother and father.

6 Praise through the night *Read Psalm 134*

The first part of the little psalm addresses a plural, while the conclusion (the last verse) addresses a singular. It seems likely that it is a dialogue. First a single cantor calls to the temple ministers (or perhaps a more general congregation) at nightfall, and then they make answer to him.

The cantor calls to 'all you servants of the Lord, that stand in the house of the Lord in the nights'. These may be especially the priestly orders that have duties in the great temple-complex of gates, courts and buildings at night-times, particularly in the festal season with its nocturnal ceremonies. They 'stand' or 'wait', ready to do whatever service the Lord requires of them.

Our singer is calling on them to 'bless the Lord'—to praise him with warm and grateful hearts. He calls on them to raise their hands towards the inner shrine, the 'Holy of Holies', the place of the Ark; here was symbolized the focus of the divine presence on earth, a place for the utmost awe, yet loved also as the fount of God's mercy and life-giving grace: 'Lift up your hands towards the holy presence, and bless the Lord!'

To this day in the Middle East, you may hear in home or street or field the gracious custom of dialogue—the giving of thanks or blessing, and the gracious reply, all steeped in the sense of the generous and compassionate heart of God. It was natural for such dialogue to sound also in the words of worship. So we hear from the 'servants of the Lord' a choral response to the cantor: 'The Lord bless you from Zion, (he who is) maker of heaven and earth!'

The call and response happily echo a deeper level of dialogue, where heartfelt praise and thanksgiving to God are answered by his further blessing. And the awesome meaning of the holy dwelling is shown with the final words: here is met the One who first made and ever makes the heaven and the earth—the world of which we have some knowledge, and the world which is as yet beyond our minds and senses. It is something to encourage us in Advent! Those who wait for the Lord, alert to do his will even through time of darkness, turned to his presence with thankful praise, such will receive blessing from the Creator—blessing that makes fruitful, and in the end means life in his presence for ever.

GUIDELINES

The weeks of Advent are a special opportunity to renew our prayers and intercessions and to turn to the Lord in readiness for his coming in the wonder of Christmas. Verses from the psalms have shown us how this turning to him can be a kind of waiting. Such waiting for him acknowledges his utter supremacy and overshadowing reality. It is an expression of trust, a confidence in his faithful love. It is held in sympathy with those who suffer long ordeals, those who sink in the mouth of destruction; and it recalls the suffering of Christ, which now undergirds all our hope.

It is indeed full of hope, just as the pilgrims, still far from Jerusalem, had in their heart that final ascent to the vision of God. The hopeful heart is also ready to bless and praise the Lord, to make that music ring out which brings in God's light.

The waiting must be in purity, which means a wholehearted willlingness to purge the kingdom of our heart. His forgiveness, faithful love and abundant redemption alone can raise us from the depths, and we wait for his word of grace more than watchmen wait for the morning. We pour out our heart before him, until there is a stillness and a silence, where it is enough to know his nearness. Through the weeks of Advent, we are like those who stood in readiness to serve throughout the night with hands stretched to-wards the Holy of Holies; we bless the Lord and receive from him and for all creation a blessing of true life with him.

And at last, by this waiting in sympathy, humility, faith, hope and love, we shall find him. Our waiting will have been our pilgrimage. We too will have been led by the Star to see the face of God in the Word made flesh.

O Lord our God, make us watchful and keep us faithful, as we await the coming of your Son our Lord, that we may be ready to behold his beauty and sing his praise.

Poetry in mission: Christmas and New Year readings

During the next two weeks we shall be participating in the celebrations of the birth of Jesus Christ and, for mathematical pedants, the 'real' turn of the millennium. Our readings will focus on the theme of mission and its consequence—the 'worldwide web' of the Church. The extraordinary fact that the Church exists in every country of the world (albeit in different forms and strengths) is due to God's own pioneering mission which draws us into following in his wake. This mission of God and of his worldwide Church is from everywhere to everywhere. In it evangelism, compassion and justice are intertwined for God's world. It is focused on Christ, often begins at home, wherever that may be for us, and is full of surprises as it moves outwards in the power of the Holy Spirit—from Jerusalem, Judea, Samaria and to the ends of the earth (Acts 1:8).

Most people who responded in writing to my earlier themes in *Guidelines* ('Mission' in 1991 and 'Sharing the good news' in 1994) commented on the poetry included. So this year each passage will be expounded more in poetry than prose. I wrote these 'expository poems ' in various contexts and countries over the last fifteen years. Their titles are given in the title for each day. I have used the New Revised Standard Version of the Bible.

18–24 DECEMBER   THE ADVENTURE OF GOD'S MISSION

---

1   The Church and the nations   *Read Luke 24:44–53*

Luke, the Gentile, ends his Gospel with the theme of proclaiming the good news to all nations (v. 47). Jesus emphasizes the fulfilment and understanding of the scriptures, focused in the sufferings of the Messiah, the witness of his own disciples and the promise of the Spirit. The following poem, written in Johannesburg in 1995, may be used as a congregational litany on this theme. It draws on the whole sweep of scripture, begins and ends with the Trinity and thus underlines the significance of God's own mission.

God the Father forms his people
    from out of the nations to bless the nations;
Jesus the Christ saves his people
    from out of the nations to bless the nations;
The Holy Spirit draws his people
    from out of the nations to bless the nations.

Abraham called
    from out of the nations, the people are blessed;
Moses leads
    from out of a nation, a people oppressed;
David fights
    against the nations, the people assured;
Isaiah speaks
    to lighten the nations, the people restored.
Jesus dies
    betrayed by the people, for the people;
Jesus dies
    pierced by the nations, for the nations.
Jesus raised
    the people remade, the nations reproached;
Paul proclaims
    the people reshaped, the nations rejoice;
John sees
    *the people redeemed, regathered from every
    tribe, tongue, people and nation.*

Source of the Church,
    Desire of the nations;
Head of the Church,
    Judge of the nations;
Breath of the Church,
    Light of the nations;
Father, Son and Holy Spirit,
    Renew your Church to bless your nations.

2   Profit and loss   *Read Luke 3:3–17*

John the Baptist, the prophet in the wilderness, introduces the
summary phrase 'repentance' and 'the forgiveness of sins' that we
saw Jesus using yesterday at the end of Luke's Gospel. I wrote the
following exposition in 1987 while on the staff of St Andrew's
Theological and Development College, Kabare, in the foothills of
Mount Kenya. The founder of the college, Dr David Gitari (now
Archbishop), was at the forefront of challenging issues of injustice
at local and national levels.

John is just the right man for the job,
which is, after all,
one of justice and righteousness.

Savile Row clothes aren't suitable,
nor is aftershave;
the dust and smell of the desert hang about him;
so do the people.

The word of the Lord, silent for so long,
At last is heard again: 'It's time to change!'

Not a polite call, in this waste land,
of 'Time, gentlemen, please';
Not 'Time to leave for tomorrow is another day'
—for it probably isn't!

But 'The crisis has come. This is it.
Here is he who comes after me.'

Not 'You can't change the world,
that's just the way it is.'
But the specific question 'Is it just, the way it is?'

The health of the poor in Britain rots
  improve housing and benefits;
The hunger and debt of the world mounts
  trade fairly and justly;

The inside of the stock market collapses
  deal honestly and openly;
Star wars astronomically cost the earth
  be content with present defence.

His shout demands, 'Time to change,
turn around, you can't go on.'
Not a casual 'Take it or leave it'
But a crucial 'Take it or be left—like the chaff.
And don't you try the old school tie;
Trees are judged by fruits, not roots.'

3 Revolutionary love   *Read Luke 6:20–36*

In Luke's Gospel, Jesus' 'blessings' are echoed by his 'woes' and
thus help to define his sayings more clearly than in Matthew's
Gospel (e.g. the meaning of 'the poor'). His sermon on the plain
(v. 17) continues with an uncompromising missionary challenge
to all cultures. I have yet to discover a culture in the world
in which it is natural to 'love your enemy'. Perhaps this is the
most revolutionary saying of Jesus. Most of Jesus' hearers would
have understood the enemy as referring to Roman soldiers.
Today's poem, written in Kenya during Holy Week in 1987,
begins with a reference to Acts 17:6 concerning Silas and Paul in
Thessalonica.

Turning the world upside down,
is the charge against Silas and Paul:
Turning its values the right way up,
is the Kingdom's promise and call.

Invitations to a glorious feast
mean more to the hungry and poor,
and to others who have the least,
than to the rich, well known and well fed,
who prefer their own company instead.

Love for those who like you is ordinary;
Love for those who are like you, narcissistic;

Love for those who are unlike you, extraordinary;
Love for those who dislike you, revolutionary.

Revenge surrenders to evil by reflecting violence:
But, like a bad coin kept and not passed on,
like lightning conducted safely to earth,
Love neutralizes evil, by absorbing violence.

Pray for the rival who threatens you;
Pray for the adversary blocking you;
Pray for the opponent who slanders you;
Pray for the antagonist provoking you.

You only love the Father
as much as you love your worst enemy.
For your love is to be merciful and free,
indiscriminate, spontaneous,
uncalculatingly generous;
When all is said and done—
like Father, like Son.

4   Coracle prayer   *Read Luke 5:1–11*

Jesus' call to the first disciples, to join him in his mission, is overwhelming in terms of demand, result and response. He meets them where they are—at work—asks for some help and issues a surprising command. Simon Peter is astounded at the miraculous catch of fish, recognizes his need of partners to help him and then leaves everything (a typical emphasis in Luke's Gospel) to follow in the wake of the Messiah. Think through how these various aspects of the story can be applied to cross-cultural mission today. Tracing further this theme of the sea, there are also other stories in the Gospels which may illuminate our own missionary calling.

A bicentenary conference of the Church Mission Society in 1999 near Derby was entitled the Coracle Event. The aim was to discover new directions for the CMS. The conference theme centred around Saint Columba (521–597) setting out in his coracle from Ireland, not knowing exactly where he was going, but trusting the wind of the Spirit. Columba ended up in his little boat at Iona, an island off the west coast of Scotland. He founded a monastery there, which formed the launching point of many missionary journeys amongst the Picts. Some people were uneasy with this 'drift of the Spirit' concept, so I wrote the following prayer-poem about Christ and the sea. Christ sends us from one shore, is with us in the boat on our journey and is already ahead of us to welcome us. As well as beginning with today's text, the poem expounds the following passages concerning the sea: Mark 4:35–41; Mark 6:45–52; John 21:1–14.

> Lord Jesus Christ,
> Teacher on the shore
>   who calls and overwhelms us,
> Friend in the boat
>   who sleeps and saves us,
> Mystery on the water
>   who prays and surprises us,
> Stranger on the other shore
>   who rises to welcome us,
> Guide our coracle across. Amen

5   First written Gospel   Read John 19:17–22

The themes of testimony and trial are woven throughout the fourth Gospel. Who is on trial in this passage? Is it Jesus, the Holy One, or Pilate, who is afraid that if he sets Jesus free he himself will be brought to trial before the emperor? The leaders of the Jews have already condemned themselves for blasphemy out of their own mouths: 'We have no king but Caesar.'

Most modern scholars consider that Mark was the first written Gospel. However, maybe we can see a supreme irony in Pilate's order concerning the 'title' written above the cross of Christ. Perhaps he who condemned Jesus wrote the first 'Gospel'—to the Jews first, but also to the Gentiles, since it was written in Hebrew, Latin and Greek for *all* to see. This poem was written on Good Friday in 1999 in Cambridge.

Jesus the Sacred, tried before Pilate;
Pilate the scared—trial before Caesar:
Jesus, entitled to justice from Rome,
Entitled by Pilate 'The King of the Jews'.

First written Gospel, translated for all,
Title deeds of the Kingdom of God;
Proclaimed to the city, unchanging Word,
'What is written is written', bequeathed to the world.

6   The point of the nails   *Read Luke 23:32–47; 24:36–43*

The inscription above the cross is again mentioned in today's reading from Luke's Gospel (23:38). Here it provokes mocking and scoffing: the message of the cross across the whole world has also often met with similar responses. God's way of eradicating ruthless sin once and for all is no easy matter: it is rooted in the body of his innocent Son. Three times in Luke's story of the cross, Jesus is declared innocent (23:4, 41, 47).

As their King, Jesus represents and sums up his people, even to the point of *being* his people, suffering as they had done historically under various pagan empires. Jesus fulfils his own command that we saw earlier in the week about loving enemies (v. 34).

Luke stresses the physicality of Jesus' transformed body (v. 42): this, however, is no mere resuscitation, but glorious resurrection— new life for old, which also relates to his people. This was written on Good Friday in 1987 at Kabare, in Kenya.

Sins aren't erased by a finger pushing the cancel button:
They're absorbed by a body pushed around and broken.

Surrounded by mocking curiosity,
Vindictive invective, derisive frivolity,
Jesus dies—declared innocent
By Governor, guerrilla and soldier.

As bread is his body and wine is his blood,
He, King of the Jews, is his people.
His death crowns their pain under pagan regimes:
He is smashed for their sins and the nations' gain.

He is raised with a transformed body,
Not as a flimsy ghost;
Not like a thin carbon-copy,
Nor even the original returned in the post.

He is raised to glorious new life,
Not back into the same,
Not like Lazarus his friend,
Who has to die again.

As the Jews were his crucified flesh,
So the Church is his glorified body.

GUIDELINES

As we look back over this week's readings, it may be helpful to respond by offering ourselves to the adventure of God's mission. There is an intriguing question: 'How do you make God smile?' The answer may be 'You tell him your plans.'

I wrote the following three prayers as a focus for our response to the Kingdom of God, the strangeness of God and the foolishness of God (1 Corinthians 1:18–25).

Our Father,
You are for turning;
turning us round
*   upside down,*
*   inside out,*
help us to give ourselves
to your revolution of
challenge and love,
through him who called for
turning and trust,
Jesus Christ our Lord,
Amen

Our Father,
you are a wild God,
*   yet we try to tame you;*
you exiled your people,
*   gave up your Son,*
*   raised up a convict,*
*   for our welcome home:*
you are a free God,
*   yet we try to cage you.*
Amen

Our Father,
you are great and glorious;
but to this twisted world
your wisdom and power
seem stupid and feeble:
grant us your insight,
your subtlety and love,
to show you to people
as you really are,
focused in your Son,
Jesus Christ our Lord,
Amen

25–31 DECEMBER   GOD'S ALL-EMBRACING MISSION

1   The gospel of the song   *Read John 1:1–14*

Mission often involves crossing boundaries, and God's worldwide, multicoloured Church is made up of many cultures. The traditional Christmas Day Gospel reading is not usually seen as a daring attempt at cross-cultural communication but that is what it is, by both God and the author. When the Word became flesh, God crossed the widest cultural gap in the universe. As the author of the fourth Gospel tries to interpret the good news to both Jews and Greeks, he chooses a metaphor that is full of meaning for both—the Word. In the Hebrew scriptures God *said*, 'Let there be light' (Genesis 1) and the heavens were made by the word of the Lord (Psalm 33:6). In popular Greek philosophical thought, the Word (*Logos*) was the meaning of the universe, the reason, the mind, the first principle behind everything. The author uses and infuses these ideas with his own focus—the Word is *personal* and, astonishingly, became flesh. In many ways, this is a crude term that implies something low and frail. Thus God shows us that 'matter' does in fact matter.

While in Kenya in 1985 I remember teaching on the doctrine of Christ—that Jesus was fully divine and fully human; not half and half, but fully both and fully integrated. I hit on the metaphor of 'the song' to illustrate this. A song is made up of words (divinity) and music (humanity) and, when sung, these two interweave together inextricably.

In the beginning were the Words,
*   and the Words were the Poet's,*
*   and were part of Him:*
*   lively and brilliant.*

And the Words became music,
*   and were sung,*
*   full of beauty and freedom.*

We have heard the Song,
*   and been utterly moved,*
*   again and again.*

We had read poetry before,
*   but beauty and freedom*
*   came through this Song.*

No one has ever seen the Poet:
*   this one Song, which is in His heart,*
*   has shown Him to us.*

2   Mandela beyond imagining   *Read Galatians 3:23–29*

Paul, in an early letter, is writing to the church he founded in Galatia. He has stressed the crucial importance of Jewish and Gentile Christians *both* being accepted by God on account of their faith in Jesus alone (v. 26). Keeping the Jewish law (focused in the issue of circumcision) does not contribute to their acceptance and salvation. Therefore, in Christ and before God, there is profound unity across racial barriers—which Paul also extends to issues of gender and slavery (v. 28).

Racial unity and justice are fundamental concerns in God's mission across the world. In 1986 the Dutch Reformed Church in South Africa repudiated its previous theological backing for apartheid. After pressure from within the country and from around the world, in February 1990 I heard on the radio in Kenya the joy of Nelson Mandela's release. The next day I wrote the following poem, which is based on this text in Galatians and on two photo images—the one of the young lawyer, with the angled parting in his hair, famous on student posters and T shirts; the other of the released prisoner which proclaimed good news on the front covers of newspapers throughout the world.

Before nineteen eighty six,
Theology in the Reformed Church
Was mistakenly myth-taken
Double Dutch and in a State.

People on whom God had set His stamp
Were stamped upon;
That which God had joined together,
People put asunder.

Then came pressure from the Spirit
Through the Word,
Through the people,
Through the nations.

Abusing the image
Insults the Original;
That which had been kept apart,
Tied together now by God.

February nineteen ninety. Behold the man,
Whose image froze a generation ago.
Has he changed? Will we know him?
President elect, but for election!
Here they come! Which one is he?

The one with Winnie's hand in his left,
Saluting the crowd with the fist of his right.

The image and likeness of the Creator
Oppressed in black, distorted in white;
The image of a captured lawyer
Stamped on T-shirts for the fight;
Now the release of a camera shutter,
Captures the image of a regal elder—
Reproduced in black and white.

3 Jesus goes underground   *Read 1 Peter 3:13–22*

This letter was written to the churches of the Roman provinces that were situated in the northern half of Asia Minor. It encouraged those churches to holiness of living and patience in suffering, following the example of Jesus Christ. Verses 18–19 and 22 contain fragments of a poem or hymn, comparable to other poems about Christ found elsewhere in the New Testament (e.g. Philippians 2:6–11; Colossians 1:15–20; Ephesians 2:14–16). Verse 15 has a powerful message for mission throughout the ages. It is an exhortation to authentic witness in the face of challenge, with the emphasis on 'gentleness and reverence'.

What is unique in this passage is the strange concept of Christ preaching to the spirits of those in prison, who had died before having an opportunity to hear the good news. The question of the unevangelized is as sensitive now as it was then. The text is reflected in the phrase of the Apostles' Creed, 'He descended to the dead', and is sometimes referred to as the 'harrowing of hell' (a doctrine of particular importance in the Eastern Orthodox churches). Too much may have been built on these verses, but the following poem, written in 1993, is a modern mythical reinterpretation. After observing various people on a London Underground train, who seemed to be imprisoned in various ways, I imagined Jesus bringing the good news to them.

> She listens to her Walkman
>   living in another world,
>   ignoring her neighbour as herself.
> He reads the Sun
>   immersed in actors' lives,
>   washing his mind with soap.
> They do not touch,
>   insulated, isolated;
>   marriage withdrawal symptoms.
> She scrunches monster munches,
>   monosodium glutamate;
>   bags of tasty emptiness.
> He's stuck in sniffing glue,
>   addicted to cheap death;
>   nobody knows the trouble he's in.
>
> To bring them to their senses and together,
> Jesus goes Underground.
>
> He grabs the tube of glue
>   and breathes the breath of God.
> He throws the packet away
>   and gives her bread.
> He joins their hands in his
>   and brings them warmth.
> He folds the sun in half
>   and beams a smile.
> He slips the headphones from her ears
>   and shares his news.

4   The image of her Father   *Read Acts 2:1–17*

Pentecost is the New Testament word for the Feast of Weeks, when the wheat harvest was celebrated by a one-day festival, during which specific sacrifices were made. This festival was fifty days after the Passover. Luke stretches language to describe this empowering baptism with the Holy Spirit (Acts 1:5) and pioneering preaching.

The disciples spoke in tongues, praising God, and Peter proclaimed the word to interpret this amazing event, showing how it related to Jewish prophecy (Joel 2:28–32). A crowd had gathered, made up of Jews from all parts of the Empire who were in Jerusalem for the festival. Luke is typically specific in his bubbling, tumbling, rushing list of nations (vv. 9–11), which is a foretaste of the worldwide Church (v. 41).

The following poem, called 'The Image of her Father', took shape as I prepared a sermon on this passage under the title the 'Birth of the Church'. This was after the birth of Miriam, our second daughter, in inner city London in 1984. I wondered who the Church's mother was, how the disciples following Jesus on the road to Jerusalem related to the Church, and how the birth involved Good Friday and Easter as well as Pentecost.

For many years in Israel's womb
The embryo grows, the Church of Christ:
First the Head, then the Body,
The Son of Man includes the many.

For hours upon a Roman cross
The Church's birth begins in blood:
Crucified with Christ her Head,
Constricted by the love of God.

The third day, from a gaping tomb,
The Church emerges urgently:
Risen again with Christ her life,
Released, relieved, the joy of God.

The fiftieth day, with tongues of flame,
She breathes the Spirit, cries the word:
Conceived, inspired with Christ, she grows,
The heir of all, the child of God.

5 Facing the image *Read 2 Corinthians 3:12–18; 4:1–6*

We continue with the concept of reflecting the image of God. In this letter, Paul is writing to the church in Corinth and contrasts his missionary ministry with the style of his detractors who have questioned his apostleship. In this passage he also daringly makes the contrast with Moses, who was afraid that his followers would see that the shining glory was fading from his face (Exodus 34 reinterpreted). Under the new covenant there is *continual* gazing and transformation into the Lord's likeness (3:18).

He then goes on to defend the integrity and openness of his and Timothy's ministry (cf. 2 Corinthians 1:1), insisting that they are not proclaiming themselves but Jesus as Lord. Using a powerful word, they are in fact the 'slaves' of their Corinthian brothers and sisters (4:5). If only Paul's example had been followed throughout the expansion of the Church! Chapter 4 verse 6 picks up again the concept of 'the face'. It focuses the essence of mission and of Christ's intimate relationship with God the creator and redeemer (Genesis 1:3 and Isaiah 60:1–2). There is a double reflective shining from God—in the missionaries and in the face of Christ.

The following litany, *Facing the Image*, was written in 1997 in Kingston, Jamaica. This was during a consultation which was looking at one of the themes of the Lambeth Conference 1998, 'Called to Full Humanity'.

Formed in the image and likeness of God,
    We rejoice;
Fired by violence and facing away,
    We recoil;
Defaced, despairing, curved in on ourselves,
    We cry;
Remaking, repairing, curved into the world,
    You come, the Image of God.

With compassion, forgiveness, restoring the image,
> *You heal;*
With powerfully piercing, incisive insight,
> *You teach;*
With passion and proverb and practical story,
> *You preach.*

Facing Jerusalem, challenging temple,
> *You suffer;*
Surfacing from the depths of death,
> *You're raised;*
Infusing, renewing, the image refacing,
> *You pour out the fiery Spirit of God.*

Being transfigured into your likeness,
> *From glory to glory;*
With unveiled face, we face God's Image,
> **Reflecting the light of the knowledge of God**
> **Seen in your face,**
> *Jesus our Lord.*

6 Turning point *Read Romans 13:11–14*

Our last passage for 2000 (the real turn of the millennium?) concerns an appeal to turn from the old life to the new. Paul is writing to the Romans from Corinth. He has not yet visited Rome but knows many of the members of the church there and, in this letter, sets out the heart of gospel of God, which unites Jews and Gentiles together through faith in Christ. He now gives an urgent ethical appeal in the light of the approaching judgment of God. He contrasts the life of quarrelling and sexual licence with new life in Christ.

It was through reading this passage that Augustine (354–430) was converted. In his autobiography, *Confessions*, he records his famous prayer, 'Give me chastity and continence, but not yet.' He describes his agony of decision concerning conversion and baptism and how the singing of a child nearby—'Pick it up and read'—prompts him to open the scriptures.

The following poem was written at Yale University in 1996,

sparked off by the first chapter of Nicholas Wolterstorff's book *Divine Discourse*, which begins with Augustine in the garden.

> *Stalking in the garden in the heat of the moment,*
> *Reflecting on complexity of voluntary movement,*
> *Slunk in listless and leaden despair,*
> *Tangled, contorted and tearing his hair,*
> *Rapping his head and wrapping his knees,*
> *Rabidly ravaging under the trees,*
> *Wanting to wait and waiting to want,*
> *Weighing the longing of laying and font,*
> *Augustine hears the Word of the Lord*
> *Drifting, insisting, the voice of a child:*
> *'Tolle, lege: take it and read.*
> *Tolle, lege: take it and read.'*
> *Vocative discourse spoken by God,*
> *Evocative sing-song challenge of a child.*

> *Turning and turning he opens to read*
> *The Word of the Lord in the words of St Paul:*
> *'Lust and debauchery, revelry, rivalry,*
> *Now is the time to wake from your sleep.'*
> *Eloquent professor professes his call.*

> *Now, no procrastination, delay;*
> *Later is now, tomorrow today.*

GUIDELINES

We conclude this theme of God's mission and his worldwide Church with a focus on the Bible. I wrote this final litany at a conference in Canterbury in 1993 on the theme of the Anglican Communion and Scripture.

In the beginning was the Word

God spoke his Word through
   Abraham and Moses,
   Deborah and Hannah,
   Samuel and David,
   Isaiah, Zechariah.
It is written   it is written.
And the Word became flesh.

God spoke his Word through
   Mary and Elizabeth,
   Simeon and Anna,
   Peter and Paul,
   Matthew and Johanna.
It is written   it is written.

God speaks his Word in
   Urdu and Tamil,
   Xhosa and Hausa,
   Spanish and English,
   Mandarin and Maori.
It is read   it is read.

   In the beginning was the Word
And the Word became flesh.

It is written   it is read,
It is old   it is new,
It is God's   it is true.

Further reading

David Bosch, *Transforming Mission*, Orbis Books, 1991.

John Stott et al., *The Anglican Communion and Scripture*, Regnum, 1996.

Kwame Bediako, *Christianity in Africa: The Renewal of a Non-Western Religion*, Edinburgh University Press/Orbis Books, 1995.

Guidelines © BRF 2000

The Bible Reading Fellowship
Peter's Way, Sandy Lane West, Oxford, OX4 5HG
ISBN 1 84101 107 X

Distributed in Australia by:
Willow Connection, PO Box 288, Brookvale, NSW 2100.
Tel: 02 9948 3957; Fax: 02 9948 8153;
E-mail: info@willowconnection.com.au
Available also from all good Christian bookshops in Australia.
For individual and group subscriptions in Australia:
Mrs Rosemary Morrall, PO Box W35, Wanniassa, ACT 2903.

Distributed in New Zealand by:
Scripture Union Wholesale, PO Box 760, Wellington
Tel: 04 385 0421; Fax: 04 384 3990; E-mail: suwholesale@clear.net.nz

Distributed in South Africa by:
Struik Book Distributors, PO Box 193, Maitland 7405, Cape Town
Tel: 021 551 5900; Fax: 021 551 1124; E-mail: enquiries@struik.co.za

Distributed in the USA by:
The Bible Reading Fellowship, PO Box 380, Winter Park,
Florida 32790-0380
Tel: 407 628 4330 or 800 749 4331; Fax: 407 647 2406;
E-mail: brf@biblereading.org; Website: www.biblereading.org

Publications distributed to more than 60 countries

Printed in Denmark

BRF MINISTRY APPEAL RESPONSE FORM

Name _____

Address _____

_____ Postcode _____

Telephone _____ Email _____

(tick as appropriate)

☐ I would like to support BRF's ministry with a regular donation by standing order (please complete the Banker's Order below).

☐ I am a UK taxpayer. Please send me a Deed of Covenant (enabling BRF to reclaim from the government the tax you have paid on your covenant)

Standing Order – Banker's Order

To the Manager, Name of Bank/Building Society _____

Address _____

_____ Postcode _____

Sort Code _____ Account Name _____

Account No _____

Please pay Royal Bank of Scotland plc, London Drummonds Branch, 49 Charing Cross, London SW1A 2DX (Sort Code 16-00-38), for the account of BRF A/C No. 00774151

The sum of _____ pounds on ___ /___ /___ (insert date your standing order starts) and thereafter the same amount on the same day of each month until further notice.

Signature _____ Date _____

Single donation

☐ I enclose my cheque/credit card/Switch card details for a donation of

£5 £10 £25 £50 £100 £250 (other) £ _____ to support BRF's ministry

Credit/ Switch card no. ☐☐☐☐☐☐☐☐☐☐☐☐☐☐☐☐☐☐☐

Expires ☐☐ ☐☐   Issue no. of Switch card ☐☐☐

Signature _____ Date _____

(Where appropriate, on receipt of your donation, we will send you a Gift Aid form)

☐ Please send me information about making a bequest to BRF in my will.

Please detach and send this completed form to: Richard Fisher, Chief Executive, BRF, Peter's Way, Sandy Lane West, OXFORD OX4 5HG.
BRF is a Registered Charity (No.233280)

BIBLE READING RESOURCES PACK

A pack of resources and ideas to help to promote Bible reading in your church is available from BRF. The pack which will be of use at any time during the year includes sample editions of the notes, magazine articles, leaflets about BRF Bible reading resources and much more. Unless you specify the month in which you would like the pack sent, we will send it immediately on receipt of your order. We greatly appreciate your donations towards the cost of producing the pack (without them we would not be able to make the pack available) and we welcome your comments about the contents of the pack and your ideas for future ones.

This coupon should be sent to:

The Bible Reading Fellowship
Peter's Way
Sandy Lane West
Oxford OX4 5HG

Name _____

Address _____

_____

_____ Postcode _____

Please send me _____ Bible Reading Resources Pack(s)

Please send the pack now/ in_____ (month).

I enclose a donation for £_____ towards the cost of the pack.

The Bible Reading Fellowship is a Registered Charity

GUIDELINES SUBSCRIPTIONS

❏ I would like to give a gift subscription (please complete both name and address sections below)

❏ I would like to take out a subscription myself (complete name and address details only once)

This completed coupon should be sent with appropriate payment to BRF. Alternatively, please write to us quoting your name, address, the subscription you would like for either yourself or a friend (with their name and address), the start date and credit card number, expiry date and signature if paying by credit card.

Gift subscription name _____

Gift subscription address _____

_____

_____ Postcode _____

Please send to the above, beginning with the January 2001 issue:

(please tick box)	UK	SURFACE	AIR MAIL
GUIDELINES	❏ £10.20	❏ £11.55	❏ £13.50
GUIDELINES 3-year sub	❏ £25.00		

Please complete the payment details below and send your coupon, with appropriate payment to: **The Bible Reading Fellowship, Peter's Way, Sandy Lane West, Oxford OX4 5HG**

Your name _____

Your address _____

_____

_____ Postcode _____

Total enclosed £ _____ (cheques should be made payable to 'BRF')

Payment by cheque ❏ postal order ❏ Visa ❏ Mastercard ❏ Switch ❏

Card number: ☐☐☐☐☐ ☐☐☐☐☐ ☐☐☐☐☐ ☐☐☐☐☐

Expiry date of card: ☐☐☐☐ Issue number (Switch): ☐☐☐☐

Signature (essential if paying by credit/Switch card) _____

NB: BRF notes are also available from your local Christian bookshop.

The Bible Reading Fellowship is a Registered Charity

BRF PUBLICATIONS ORDER FORM

Please ensure that you complete and send off both sides of this order form.
Please send me the following book(s):

		Quantity	Price	Total
080 4	Jesus in the Third Millennium (R. Frost)	_____	£5.99	_____
145 2	Bible Voices (A. Geering)	_____	£5.99	_____
174 6	Love is Full of Surprises (J. Hyson)	_____	£3.99	_____
030 8	PBC: 1 & 2 Samuel (H. Mowvley)	_____	£7.99	_____
070 7	PBC: Chronicles—Nehemiah (M. Tunnicliffe)	_____	£7.99	_____
031 6	PBC: Psalms 1—72 (D. Coggan)	_____	£7.99	_____
065 0	PBC: Psalms 73—150 (D. Coggan)	_____	£7.99	_____
071 5	PBC: Proverbs (E. Mellor)	_____	£7.99	_____
028 6	PBC: Nahum—Malachi (G. Emmerson)	_____	£7.99	_____
046 4	PBC: Mark (D. France)	_____	£7.99	_____
027 8	PBC: Luke (H. Wansbrough)	_____	£7.99	_____
029 4	PBC: John (R.A. Burridge)	_____	£7.99	_____
3280 0	PBC: 1 Corinthians (J. Murphy-O'Connor)	_____	£7.99	_____
012 X	PBC: Galatians and 1 & 2 Thessalonians (J. Fenton)	_____	£7.99	_____
092 8	PBC: James—Jude (F. Moloney)	_____	£7.99	_____
3297 5	PBC: Revelation (M. Maxwell)	_____	£7.99	_____

Total cost of books £ _____

Postage and packing (see over) £ _____

TOTAL £ _____

See over for payment details. All prices are correct at time of going to press, are subject to the prevailing rate of VAT and may be subject to change without prior warning.
NB: All BRF titles are also available from your local Christian bookshop.

GL0300   The Bible Reading Fellowship is a Registered Charity

PAYMENT DETAILS

Please complete the payment details below and send with appropriate payment and completed order form to:

The Bible Reading Fellowship,
Peter's Way,
Sandy Lane West,
Oxford OX4 5HG

Name _____

Address _____

_____

_____Postcode _____

Total enclosed £ _____ (cheques should be made payable to 'BRF')

Payment by cheque ❏ postal order ❏ Visa ❏ Mastercard ❏ Switch ❏

Card number: ☐☐☐☐ ☐☐☐☐ ☐☐☐☐ ☐☐☐☐

Expiry date of card: ☐☐☐☐   Issue number (Switch): ☐☐☐☐

Signature (essential if paying by credit/Switch card) _____

POSTAGE AND PACKING CHARGES				
order value	UK	Europe	Surface	Air Mail
£7.00 & under	£1.25	£2.25	£2.25	£3.50
£7.01–£30.00	£2.50	£3.50	£4.50	£6.50
Over £30.00	free	prices on request		

Alternatively you may wish to order books using the BRF telephone order hotline:
01865 748227

The Bible Reading Fellowship is a Registered Charity